A Child's Garden of Quilts

by Christal Carter

That Patchwork Place®

❧ Dedication

This book is dedicated to my mother, Bettie Williams, who gave us a warm and secure childhood by nightly tucking us into bed, listening to our prayers, and telling us she loved us. I love you, Mom, for thinking I was wonderful and encouraging my every endeavor. And I love you for allowing me to use crayons on your white percale sheets so that I would have scenery for my backyard productions. Little did you know that those hand-colored scenes would be the first form my quilts would take.

❧ Credits

Editor-in-Chief . . . . Barbara Weiland
Technical Editor . . . . Janet White
Managing Editor . . . . Greg Sharp
Copy Editor . . . . Tina Cook
Proofreader . . . . Leslie Phillips
Design Director . . . . Judy Petry
Text and Cover Designer . . . . Dani Ritchardson
Production Assistants . . . . Shean Bemis
Claudia L'Heureux
Photographer . . . . Brent Kane
Technical Illustrator . . . . Brian Metz
Illustration Assistant . . . . Lisa McKenney
Decorative Art . . . . Dani Ritchardson

That Patchwork Place
PO Box 118
Bothell, WA 98041-0118 USA

Printed in the United States of America
99 98 97 96 95 94 6 5 4 3 2 1

Library of Congress Cataloging-in-Publication Data
Carter, Christal
    A child's garden of quilts / Christal Carter.
        p.   cm.
    ISBN 1-56477-077-X :
    1. Quilting—Patterns. 2. Patchwork—Patterns.
3. Children's quilts. I. Title.
TT835.C378 1994
746.46—dc20   94-34263
                                                            CIP

❧ Acknowledgments

There are several people who deserve recognition for their help with this book. My thanks go to:

Barbara Ford, for machine quilting (with tight deadlines) five of my quilts and adding her own special touches.

Irene Chang, for quilting the "Guardian Angel" quilt in the midst of the Northridge earthquake!

My dear friend Eileen Adams, who helped by hanging quilts and taking photos.

My daughter, Catrina Carter, and friend, Judy Gagner, for their great design suggestions.

My husband, Bill, for all the computer help and the bouquets of flowers to encourage me.

My daughter, Carin Christerson, for her original "Mother Goose" drawing and for the use of her "Cat-o-lantern" design and quilt.

Nancy J. Martin and the wonderful and efficient staff at That Patchwork Place.

Bonnie Leman, for first suggesting to me a book of children's designs.

MISSION STATEMENT

WE ARE DEDICATED TO PROVIDING QUALITY PRODUCTS THAT ENCOURAGE CREATIVITY AND PROMOTE SELF-ESTEEM IN OUR CUSTOMERS AND OUR EMPLOYEES.

WE STRIVE TO MAKE A DIFFERENCE IN THE LIVES WE TOUCH.

That Patchwork Place is an employee-owned, financially secure company.

Contents

Introduction

Because I was the eldest of four children, and because my mother was ill as we grew up, I was responsible for many "motherly" chores. I worked at the family grocery market, helped fix meals at home, and often filled Easter baskets or Christmas stockings for the family. Now, looking back, I see why the quilts I design are so childlike and whimsical. I think I am trying to recapture a bit of my lost childhood. I love disappearing into the happy designs and becoming a child again.

The quilts in this book include a wide variety of themes and sizes. There are designs for the newborn ("Bundle of Joy," "Mother Goose's Garden," and "Humpty Dumpty"), quilts for preschoolers ("The Three Little Kittens" and the "Lions, Tigers, and Bears" trio), and designs for youth ("Stop and Go" and "The Old Oak Tree"). There are even designs for holidays and celebrations ("Cat-o-lantern," "Christmas Nativity," and "Guardian Angel"). The quilts range in size from small, for the beginning quilter, to large, for the advanced quilter.

As you make the quilts featured in this book, I hope that you fill them with stitches of love, whether they are for someone special to you or for yourself.

General Guidelines

Materials and Equipment

Rotary Cutter and Mat

The indispensable rotary cutter not only saves time for quilters but also improves accuracy. It is a real must for the patterns in this book. I prefer to use the larger blade. If you cannot find one in a store near you, they are available through mail order.

The rotary cutter cannot be used without a mat. These mats are specially made for rotary cutters and will last for years. I have been using the same mat for thirteen years, and it seems to be none the worse for wear. I prefer mats with premarked grids to help ensure straight cutting.

Sharp Fabric-Cutting Scissors

A pair of good scissors is a wonderful investment for any type of sewing. You may also want to purchase a whetstone for scissor sharpening. A good shop will sell whetstones along with the scissors and should take the time to show you how to use them. I sharpen my own scissors, saving time and money.

Paper-Cutting Scissors

These could be a pair of old or inexpensive scissors to use for cutting freezer paper and patterns. Cutting paper will dull a good pair of scissors.

Embroidery Scissors

A pair of small, sharp scissors is helpful in cutting small pieces of fabric for appliqué and embroidery work and for snipping quilting threads during hand quilting.

Sewing Machine

All of the projects in this book can be pieced by machine. A good-quality machine is invaluable. Before beginning any machine work, make sure the machine is clean and oiled. Replace the needle after every eight hours of sewing. Use a needle for "fine" fabrics with these small Log Cabin blocks.

Marking Tools

Water-soluble fabric marking pens
Number 2 lead pencils
White dressmaker's pencil for marking dark
fabrics
Colored pencils to color quilt plans and blocks

Rulers

You will need a clear acrylic quilter's ruler to cut strips. Rulers come in a variety of widths and lengths. I prefer a width of 3" and a length of 24", with lines marked every ¼" to ½". Most of the strips you will cut for these projects require 1"-wide strips.

It is also helpful to have a square plastic ruler, such as the 6" Bias Square® or 4" Baby Bias Square®, for squaring your blocks.

Other Equipment

Light box. This wooden box, fitted with a clear glass or acrylic top and a light underneath, is used for tracing. Make your own by putting a small lamp under a glass-topped coffee table. Some of my students use their dining table, separated in the middle where the leaves would go. Cover the gap with a piece of heavy glass and put a lamp under the table. It is a good height for tracing.

Iron and ironing board

Hoops. Both embroidery and quilting hoops are needed for these projects.

Full-size quilting frame. This is optional but is helpful for hand quilting or while basting or pinning quilt tops in preparation for hand or machine quilting.

Needles. You will need the following for the projects in this book:

Small sharps for appliqué
Quilting needles for hand quilting
Machine needles
Embroidery needles

Thimbles

Interfacing. Keep both fusible and nonfusible on hand.

Thread. You will need the following types of thread:

Machine sewing thread
Embroidery floss
Quilting thread
Pearl cotton

Tracing paper

Clear template plastic or cardboard. This is used for making templates.

Black permanent felt-tip pen, fine point

Roll of freezer paper. Available in grocery stores, this is used for freezer-paper appliqué.

Miscellaneous notions. Items such as bias tape, quilt batting, and cording are needed for some patterns.

🌿 Fabrics

Fabric Content

As a rule, 100% cotton fabrics are the best choices for the patterns in this book. The fabrics should be colorfast and similar in weight and texture.

For hand appliqué work and blind-stitch machine appliqué, 100% cotton is preferable. It is easy to work with when folding under the raw edges. If you are not sure of a particular fabric's fiber content, try the following quick test. Tightly pinch a folded edge of the fabric and see if a crease line remains. If a line is plainly visible, the fabric will probably work well for appliqué. If no crease forms and the fabric is difficult to "finger press," it is more likely to be a cotton/synthetic blend and will be more difficult to work with.

Cotton blends are fine, however, if you plan to machine appliqué with a satin-stitch edge, because the edges do not need to be turned under. In fact, a permanent-press blend is often preferred, especially if the finished item will be washed repeatedly. A garment, for example, will come out of the dryer in great shape if the fabrics used for appliqué are cotton-polyester blends.

I sometimes break the rules by using a fabric that is more "exotic," such as the lamés I used in "Guardian Angel" on page 52. If the lamé does not already have a backing and ravels easily, press fusible interfacing to the back before cutting it into strips. Use caution with these unusual fabrics, especially if you are a novice at quiltmaking. Velvets, for example, are really too thick to combine with cotton in these small Log Cabin blocks.

Fabric Preparation

Always prewash and tumble dry fabrics. Press the prewashed and dried fabrics before starting to cut. Any time I purchase fabric, it goes directly to the laundry room before being added to my studio shelves. Fabrics often shrink or bleed, even though labeled preshrunk and colorfast. Even after washing, some dyes continue to bleed, so double-check by pressing a damp corner of the colored fabric onto a scrap of white fabric. If the fabric continues to "bleed," try to set the dye by adding 1 cup of white vinegar to a sink full of water and soaking the fabric. Rinse and test again. If the fabric continues to bleed, discard it.

Fabric Selection

For these Log Cabin picture designs, I use solids and small- to medium-scale prints that contain few colors. Very busy or large prints tend to complicate the design and draw attention to themselves. It is best if the eye is drawn to the overall picture, rather than to a particularly busy or large-scale print within the picture. The strips used in these designs are very narrow and often, with a large multicolor print, the very color you wished to emphasize is not even contained in the strip. When this happens, you lose the color grouping and blur the picture you are trying to create.

Sometimes, I use all one fabric rather than a combination of fabrics. For example, in "Christmas Nativity" on page 52, Joseph's coat, Mary's robe, and the sky are each made up of only one fabric. The resulting effect de-emphasizes the piecing and creates a unified look.

Color Groupings

Decide carefully which fabrics to include in each color group. The groups should "read" as if they are a unit. For example, the bricks in "Humpty Dumpty" are composed of three groups of red fabrics: light, medium, and dark. The fabrics in each group are similar in value and scale so that they work together as a unit. The variety of fabrics is different enough to show off the piecing, yet not so different that the bricks look choppy. The key is to achieve unity in value (darkness or lightness of a color), while combining fabrics that are slightly different so that all those little pieces show.

Also, take into consideration color groupings that border each other. Bordering groups must each be of a different value. If you place a group of medium greens next to a group of medium blues, you risk losing your picture, because colors of similar value will blend together from a distance.

The following exercise will help you learn to group fabrics according to color and value. Cut and paste ½"-wide strips of fabric onto the Sample Log Cabin on page 7, using the color combination suggested. Try to aim for a unified look to the house front but one that contrasts slightly with the house side. Both the front and the side should contrast with the roof and sky. Look at the finished sample from a distance. Did you achieve a clear picture of the house, or are there strips that are too dark or too light? Are any of the prints too large or too busy? Is the house front distinctly different from the house side?

Think of these things as you select fabrics for the color groups in these patterns. Each color group could have several similar fabrics. If you use only three fabrics, you will repeat the use of each fabric two or more times, which I do often.

To do a quick check of your fabrics, lay out each color group, overlapping fabrics by ½" (the width of the finished strips in the patterns), then look at the group from a distance. If one of the fabrics stands out "like a sore thumb," discard it and use fewer fabrics, or shop for a replacement fabric that is similar to the rest of the grouping.

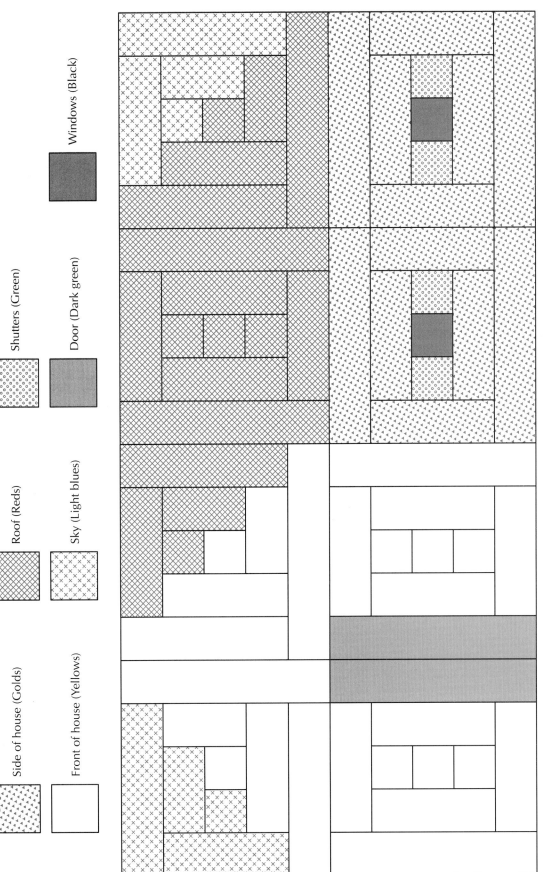

Windows (Black)

Shutters (Green)

Door (Dark green)

Roof (Reds)

Sky (Light blues)

Side of house (Golds)

Front of house (Yellows)

Sample Log Cabin

❧ *Cutting and Pressing*

Cutting

To make the blocks quickly and precisely, use a rotary cutter and mat. A good mat size is 18" x 24". The blocks are speed-pieced using 1"-wide strips of fabric. *Read through each pattern before you begin to cut your 1"-wide strips, because some of the fabrics need to be reserved for the appliqué pieces, borders, and binding strips.*

The rotary cutter will easily cut through four to six layers of fabric. Use your quilter's ruler to measure and cut strips 1" wide. Be sure to make straight cuts that are perpendicular to the fold, otherwise the strips may have a slight bias stretch. I usually fold my fabric only once (the way it comes on the bolt) and cut strips selvage to selvage. You can stack two or three fabrics, each folded once. Try to avoid folding fabric too many times, since it will often result in crooked strips as shown below.

Folding like this:

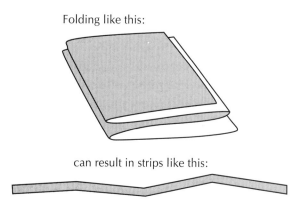

can result in strips like this:

There is no need to mark fabrics for cutting, simply run the rotary cutter along the ruler edge. If the cut is not clean and the strip is still attached here and there, you probably have a nick in the blade. Replace it with a new one. Rotary cutter blades will last a long time if you avoid hitting the ruler and any stray straight pins. Cutters should be cleaned and lightly oiled periodically. Be sure to wipe off any excess oil before cutting fabric.

Try to use the same acrylic ruler throughout a project. Also, it is a good idea to mark one edge of the ruler with paint or tape. Use the marked side of the ruler throughout the project. I have found that ruler sizes vary, even though they all have 1" measurements. The most important thing about making these blocks is not that the strips are exactly 1" wide, but that the strips are all the same size. Discard any strips that seem to be wider or narrower than the rest, as they will result in blocks that are too small or too large. Do not use the grid on your cutting mat to measure strips.

If necessary, you can mark strips and then cut with scissors, but rotary cutting saves time and improves accuracy. It is well worth the investment.

As a rule, it takes about 1 strip (1" x 44") to make one 13-piece block. One strip (1" x 44") will make 2 blocks if they have only 9 pieces. Using this guideline can help you figure the yardage required and number of strips to cut. If the pattern calls for twelve 13-piece blocks, you will need about 12" of fabric or 1/3 yard. If the pattern calls for twelve 9-piece blocks, you will need about 6" of fabric or 1/6 yard.

Example: A pattern calls for 24 blocks (13-piece blocks) of sky blues. One 13-piece block requires a whole strip of fabric cut selvage to selvage. You will need 24" of fabric to cut twenty-four 1"-wide strips. Perhaps you would like to use four different fabrics in your sky. Four divided into twenty-four is six, so you will need 6" each of four blue fabrics to equal the 24" required.

Pressing

With the narrow strips used in these Log Cabin blocks, it is essential to press each log as you go. I always use a dry iron because my fingers are so close to the pressing and the steam is a bit dangerous. Since pressing is needed often during the piecing process, keep your ironing board close.

I made a special free-standing board, which is just the right height, from an inexpensive wooden bar stool and a small wooden ironing board. I removed the short legs from the ironing board and screwed the ironing board to the top of the bar stool. (Screws go in underneath the bar stool and up into the wooden board.) The legs of the bar stool can be cut off at the desired height. Mine easily slides under my sewing table when not in use.

All seams in Log Cabin blocks are pressed away from the center square. When pressing the first double strip in the speed-piecing sequence, press away from the strip that will be the center square of the blocks. As blocks progress in the speed-piecing process, always press seams toward the new, uncut strip that has just been added. The wrong side of the block should look like this:

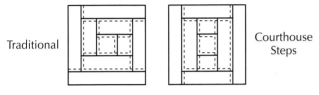

Traditional   Courthouse Steps

Wrong sides

It is also important to make sure there are no pleats or tucks. While the "logs" should not be stretched, they should be pressed all the way out; otherwise, the blocks will be too small. I always press on the right side (or top) of the blocks to prevent pleats and tucks.

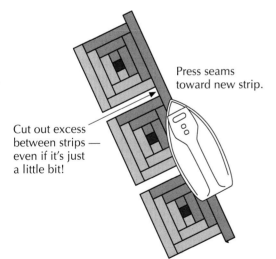

Press seams toward new strip.

Cut out excess between strips — even if it's just a little bit!

Many of my students have found it helpful to press seams while the blocks are still attached to the strip, before cutting blocks apart. This helps to keep blocks square as logs are added.

Templates

The templates on the following pages are shown full-size. Some of the blocks are Traditional Log Cabin blocks and some are Courthouse Steps blocks. There are also some unusual blocks: Off-Center and Rounded Log Cabin blocks. The Alphabet and Number blocks are specially pieced.

Traditional blocks are pieced in a clockwise order in all of my patterns. Some quilters piece their traditional blocks in a counterclockwise sequence. Either way is correct, but for the patterns in this book, piece them clockwise as shown. There are a few special blocks that require counterclockwise piecing. These are clearly indicated in the pattern section. Whenever you wish to divide a block in half diagonally, use a Traditional block.

Be sure to add ¼"-wide seam allowances to each template. The pieces are numbered to indicate the order in which strips are added to the blocks. Some blocks are 9-piece blocks (a center square with two rounds of "logs" added). Some blocks are 13-piece blocks (a center square with 3 rounds of "logs" added). Some of the Alphabet blocks have more than 13 pieces.

Courthouse Steps is another type of Log Cabin block. It is the easiest and least confusing of all the Log Cabin blocks to assemble. Since the blocks are symmetrical, it is easy to see the strip placement during piecing. They are also quick to assemble for two reasons.

First, you speed up the beginning process by sewing three strips together instead of two strips as in other block types. See page 14. Second, as the block gets larger, you can sew the two opposite strips of fabric before pressing, which saves one pressing step. Whenever I have the option of using either type of block in a design, I choose Courthouse Steps. For example, in many of the background areas that are all one color, I could use either type of block, but I always use Courthouse Steps blocks because they are easier to construct.

There are also some special blocks. The **Off-Center block** is used in "Toytime Teddy" for the nose and eye blocks. These are blocks in which logs are sewn only to two sides of the center square. This leaves the center square (piece #1) bare on two sides.

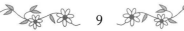

The **Alphabet and Number blocks**, as well as a few others throughout the book, are pieced in an unusual order. These blocks are always shown last in each pattern and are labeled "Unusual Blocks." The numbering in each block indicates the piecing sequence. Take your time with these special blocks, checking them often to make sure that your block matches the diagram.

The **Rounded Log Cabin block** can be made from Traditional blocks or Courthouse Steps blocks. Cutting off four corners and adding a different fabric in the corners make the block appear "rounded." The roses in "Bundle of Joy" are rounded Log Cabin blocks. Also, the feet in the "Honey Bear" quilt each have one rounded corner.

All of the blocks in this book can be made using the speed piecing methods discussed in the next section. It is much faster and easier than cutting individual templates. I suggest that you use the templates only as guidelines for the piecing sequence and finished size. Remember, your finished blocks will be squares that are ½" larger than the templates due to the ¼"-wide seam allowance all around the block. The template represents the finished size of the block after being sewn into the quilt.

🦋 *Traditional Blocks*

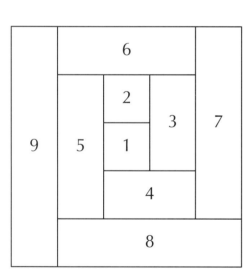

2½" Block

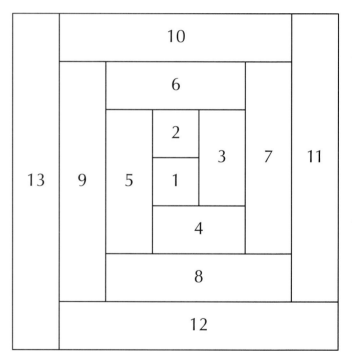

3½" Block

🦋 *Courthouse Steps Blocks*

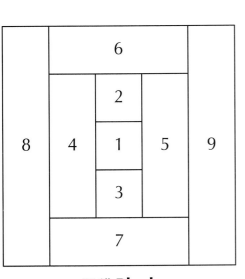

2½" Block

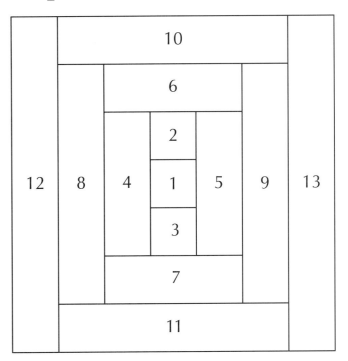

3½" Block

🦋 *Off-Center Blocks*

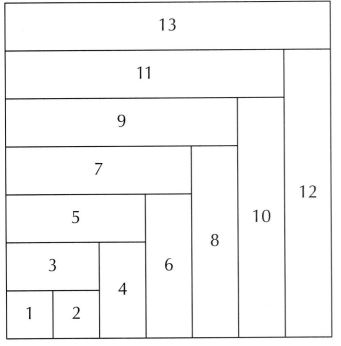

3½" Block

🦋 *Rounded Blocks*

These may be made from Traditional, Courthouse Steps, Off-Center, or unusual blocks. A Traditional block is shown here.

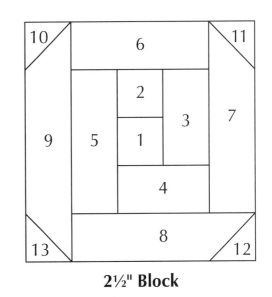

2½" Block

Speed Piecing

I recommend the use of speed piecing techniques for all of the projects in this book. There are usually several of each type and color combination of block, so making them all at once saves time.

Before beginning to speed-piece the blocks, it is a good idea to make a sample block. This will enable you to check strip width, seam allowances, and finished block size. Use ¼"-wide seam allowances for all blocks. If you have a special ¼" foot for your machine, use it. Just make sure that there is never any fabric showing outside the ¼" foot as you sew. Line the fabric up along the foot edge, just inside it.

When you have completed a sample block, compare it to the templates. Are your finished logs at least ½" wide? Check the center of the block. Is it square? Have you pressed the logs all the way out, or are there "pleats"? Is your block the right size? A 9-piece block should be 3" x 3" including seam allowances, a 13-piece block should be 4" x 4" including seam allowances, and a 17-piece block should be 5" x 5" including seam allowances.

Make the necessary adjustments and you are ready to begin speed piecing.

Speed Piecing Traditional Blocks

The following sample calls for six Traditional blocks.

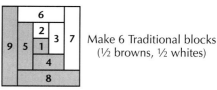

Make 6 Traditional blocks
(½ browns, ½ whites)

Look at the Traditional block. The smallest pieces are squares—the center (brown piece #1) and a piece beside the center (white piece #2). Cut a 1" x 8" strip of brown fabric and a 1" x 8" strip of white fabric. This allows 1" of fabric for each block needed plus a couple of extra inches.

With right sides together, sew the strips together along one edge, using a ¼"-wide seam allowance. Press the seam away from the center color, in this case, brown.

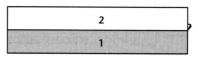

Press seams away
from center square (brown).

Basic Guidelines

- Cut selvages off of strips.
- Cut strips exactly 1" wide, straight and accurate. Discard any strips that are crooked or too wide or too narrow.
- Use straight machine stitching, with ¼"-wide seam allowances. Use 12–14 stitches per inch with a neutral-colored thread.
- Press strips after each sewing step.
- When cutting blocks apart, cut straight and perpendicular to the strip to keep blocks square.
- Do not change sewing machines, templates, or methods in the middle of a project. This may result in blocks of varying sizes.

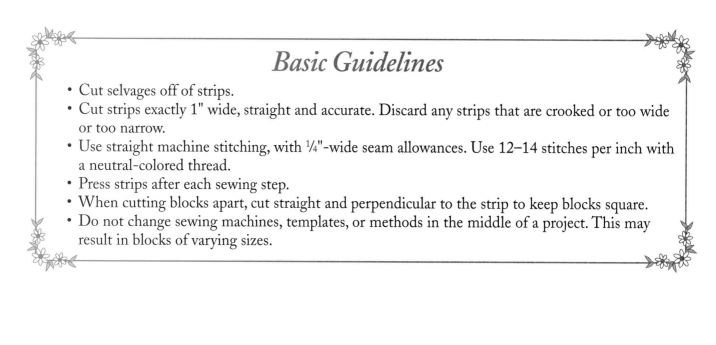

Cut the strip into 6 pieces, each 1" wide, using your ruler and rotary cutter. Now you have pieces #1 and #2 sewn together for all 6 blocks.

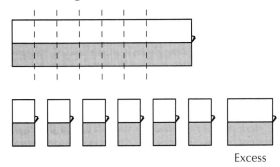

Piece #3 of the sample block is another white fabric. Choose a different white strip and lay this #3 strip on the machine with the right side facing up.

Note: With speed piecing, the new fabric strip always goes on the machine first and block pieces are laid on top of the strip.

Place the small block pieces, right side down, on the strip as shown, with piece #1 at the top of the strip and piece #2 near you. Sew ¼" from the right edge, adding blocks to the strip as you sew. You may butt the blocks together on the strip, but do not overlap them.

Note: From this point on, graphs will not indicate fabric color, only the right and wrong sides of blocks and strips. The right side is darkened; the wrong side is not.

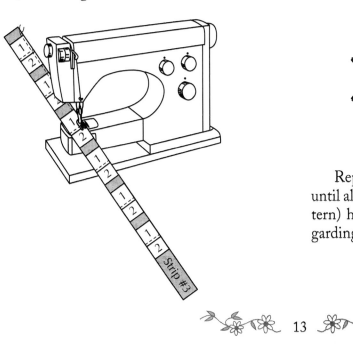

After sewing all six blocks to the strip, remove from the machine. Press the blocks with the seams toward the new uncut strip. Cut blocks apart with a rotary cutter, making sure to cut out any excess fabric between the blocks. If small amounts of excess fabric between blocks are not removed, blocks will "grow." You now have six blocks that look like this.

Piece #4 is brown. Choose a different brown strip than piece #1 and place on the machine, right side up. Place the blocks on the strip with the right side down. Always keep the piece that you added to the block last (piece #3, in this case) nearest to you as you place it on the strip. Sew the blocks to the strip. Remove from the machine, press seams toward the new uncut strip, and cut blocks apart.

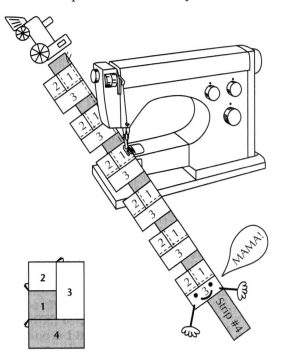

Repeat this process of sewing blocks to strips until all 9 pieces (or 13 or 17, depending on the pattern) have been added. Refer to the quilt plan regarding piece numbers and colors.

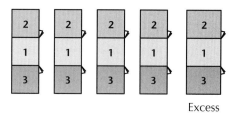

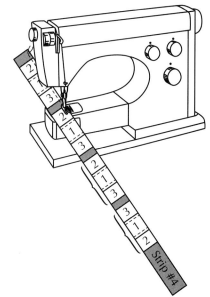

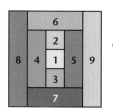

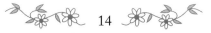

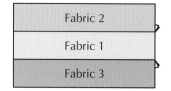

Some Helpful Hints

When working with the fabric strips and block pieces, think of the machine feed dog as a railroad track. Think of the long strips as the train and the blocks as the cargo. This helps you to remember that the strip (train) always goes on the machine (tracks) first and the cargo (blocks) are loaded onto the train. Never put the cargo under the train!

To remember how to place the blocks on the train, try to visualize this: The piece you added to the blocks last is your newest baby. (He might be the biggest, but he is the newest!) Your newest baby always wants his mama. That is you! So place the blocks on the strip with the newest baby (latest strip addition) nearest you. He is near the caboose wanting to jump off the train to you.

Speed Piecing Courthouse Steps Blocks

Look at the Courthouse Steps sample block. There are three small squares that are all the same size (pieces #1, #2, and #3). The sample exercise calls for 4 blocks, all blues. This means that you can use a variety of fabrics randomly placed.

Courthouse Steps
Make 4 blocks
(all blues).

Select three blue strips, all different, and cut them 6" long (1" for each block needed plus a couple of extra inches). Sew the three strips together as shown and press seams away from the center strip.

Fabric 2
Fabric 1
Fabric 3

Press seams away from center strip.

Cut the strip into four pieces, each 1" wide. Now you have pieced #1, #2, and #3 for all four blocks.

Excess

Select another blue strip for piece #4 (repeat a fabric if necessary.) Lay the strip, right side up, on the machine. Place the blocks, right side down, on the strip. Unlike the Traditional blocks, you do not place the piece you added last nearest you. With Courthouse Steps blocks, always place the blocks so that you will be sewing across two seams.

Blocks may be turned either way on the strip, with piece #2 or piece #3 at the top. Varying this placement will add more variety to your blocks. Butt the blocks together as you place them on the strip. Do not overlap the blocks. Sew ¼" from the right edge of the strip. Remove the blocks from the machine and press the seams toward the new, uncut strip. Cut blocks apart, removing any excess fabric between blocks. Your blocks will look like this:

Select a blue strip for piece #5. Sew the blocks to the strip as shown.

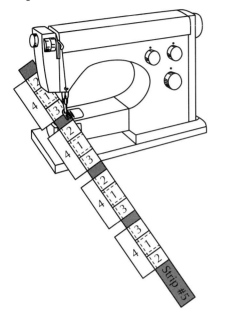

Press seams toward the new, uncut strip, and cut blocks apart. Repeat this process of sewing blocks to the strips until all 9 pieces (or 13 pieces, depending on the pattern) have been added. Refer to the quilt plan for piece numbers and colors.

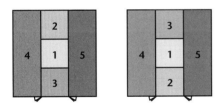

Speed Piecing Off-Center Blocks

The sample exercise calls for 5 blocks, all greens.

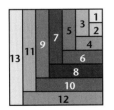

Make 5 blocks (all greens).

Cut two different 1"-wide green strips, each about 7" long (1" for each block plus a couple of extra inches). Sew the strips together with right sides facing, using a ¼"-wide seam allowance. Press the seam away from strip #1. Cut the strip into five

pieces, each 1" wide. You now have pieces #1 and #2 for all five blocks.

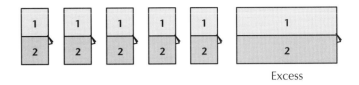

Excess

Lay another green strip on the machine. Place the blocks on the strip with piece #1 (center) at the top of the strip as shown. Sew the blocks to the strip. Press seams toward the new, uncut strip. Cut blocks apart, making sure to remove any excess fabric between strips.

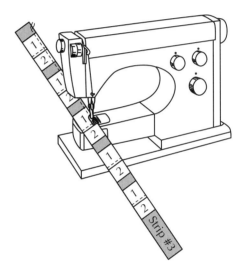

Lay a different green strip on the machine (repeat a fabric if necessary) and lay the blocks on the strip with piece #3 at the top of the strip, and the #1/#2 unit nearest you. Sew blocks to the strip. Press seams toward the new, uncut strip. Cut blocks apart.

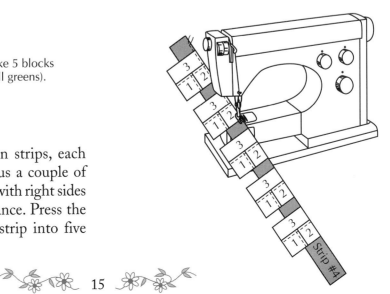

Continue adding strips to the block, making sure to add strips to only two sides of the block. This keeps piece #1 off-center, forming the Off-Center blocks. Add strips until the desired number is reached (9 or 13).

Speed Piecing Rounded Log Cabin Blocks

These are started either as Traditional Blocks or Courthouse Steps blocks. But at some point, either after 9 or 13 pieces have been added, four corners are cut off at 45° angles as shown.

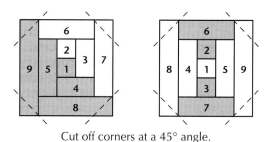

Cut off corners at a 45° angle.

These missing triangles must now be replaced with another color. Triangles could actually be cut and pieced in, but there is a speed-piecing technique that is much faster.

To Piece in the Triangles:

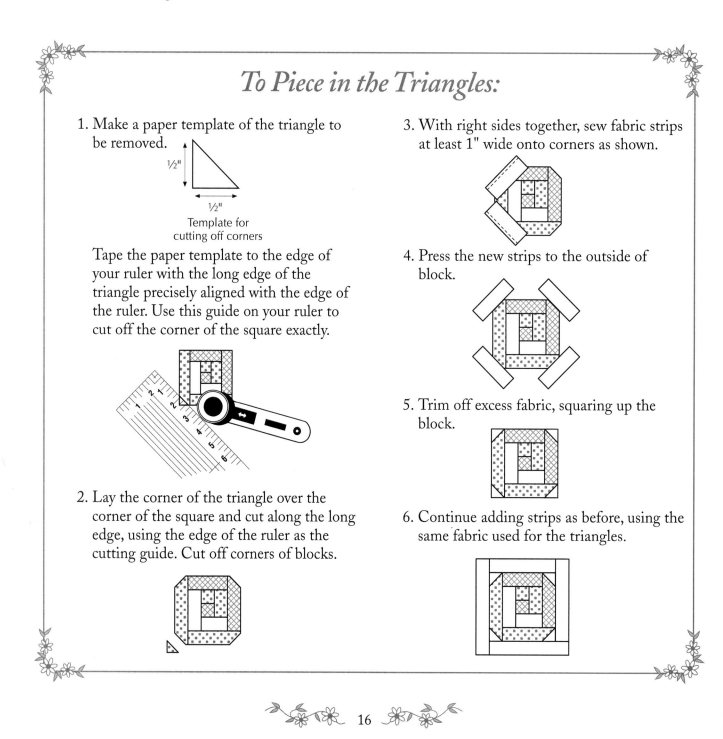

1. Make a paper template of the triangle to be removed.

½"

½"

Template for cutting off corners

Tape the paper template to the edge of your ruler with the long edge of the triangle precisely aligned with the edge of the ruler. Use this guide on your ruler to cut off the corner of the square exactly.

2. Lay the corner of the triangle over the corner of the square and cut along the long edge, using the edge of the ruler as the cutting guide. Cut off corners of blocks.

3. With right sides together, sew fabric strips at least 1" wide onto corners as shown.

4. Press the new strips to the outside of block.

5. Trim off excess fabric, squaring up the block.

6. Continue adding strips as before, using the same fabric used for the triangles.

If you have several blocks to make using the same color triangles, place the blocks on the strip as shown. This will make one corner of each block. Press and cut blocks apart. Repeat this process with all blocks for each of the corners.

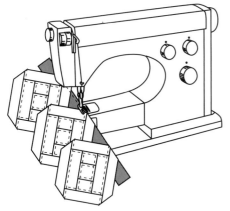

Speed Piecing Unusual Blocks

Sometimes a pattern calls for an unusual block. This means that the pieces might be added "out of order" from the normal piecing sequence. Or, there may be an extra piece added to a log. These are illustrated and are always placed last in each pattern.

Some Reasons for Imperfect Blocks

- Strips unevenly cut
- Strips cut too large or too small
- Strips cut on a slight bias and stretched during sewing or pressing
- Seam allowances too wide (over ¼") or too narrow (under ¼")
- Seam allowances unevenly sewn
- Machine needle not sharp enough
- Machine not stitching properly
- Stitch length too short or too long
- Improper pressing resulting in pleats
- Failure to press between sewing steps
- Pressing with steam, especially on fabric that was not preshrunk
- Using fabric blends
- Combining fabrics of varying weights and textures

❧ *Block Assembly*

Complete all of the individual blocks for a project before beginning to sew them together. Check to make sure all of your blocks are the same size. Blocks may be trimmed slightly if oversized. Rather than trimming from just one side, trim a little from each edge. Follow the directions for each project to assemble the blocks in rows. With "Bundle of Joy" (page 25), for example, there are more vertical than horizontal lines (notice the stork's neck), so you will assemble these blocks in vertical rows. That will ensure neat, even connections when you sew the rows together. Follow the directions with each project to assemble the blocks in horizontal or vertical rows.

When rows are sewn together vertically, press the seams between the blocks this way: seams in row 1 up, seams in row 2 down, seams in row 3 up and so on. When you sew the rows together, the seams will meet and go in opposite directions.

Note: This refers only to those seams that connect block to block, not the seams within the block.

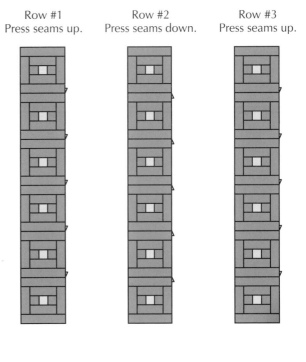

Row #1
Press seams up.

Row #2
Press seams down.

Row #3
Press seams up.

When assembling blocks in horizontal rows, as in "Humpty Dumpty" on pages 28–30, press the seams in row 1 to the right, row 2 to the left, row 3 to the right, and so on.

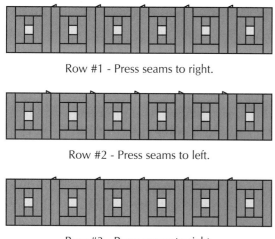

Row #1 - Press seams to right.

Row #2 - Press seams to left.

Row #3 - Press seams to right.

When you sew the rows together, always match blocks at each connecting seam. The pressed seams should go in opposite directions. If blocks do not match exactly, you can slightly stretch the smaller block to fit. If there is too much difference for them to match, you may have to adjust or even remake a block. The long seams between rows may be pressed in either direction.

Appliqué

Appliqué is the "application" or attachment of a fabric piece to a background fabric. The background may be pieced or it may be a single length of fabric. Appliqué can be done by hand or by machine. For the latest methods in machine appliqué, I suggest buying or borrowing a book on the subject. There are many new products and techniques now available to make machine work look like you have done hours of handwork. For the quilts in this book, I have used primarily hand techniques.

I use so many different appliqué methods that it is difficult to choose one "best" technique. In one quilt, I often use three different techniques because each has its own advantages and special uses.

Hand Appliqué – Method 1 – Basted

This is the method I use most often because it is fairly fast, and prebasting allows me to have some control over the pieces to be appliquéd.

1. With tracing paper and a permanent, black felt-tip pen, trace the patterns and any embroidery lines from the pattern sheet.
2. Place the traced patterns on a light box and, using a marking tool of your choice, trace the patterns and embroidery lines onto the right side of the appropriate fabrics. As you mark the fabric, be sure to leave space for 1/4"-wide seam allowances around each piece.
3. Cut out each piece of fabric, adding 1/4"-wide seam allowances to all edges as you cut. This 1/4" need not be marked or exact. Fold the seam allowance to the wrong side, exactly on the drawn line, but do not let pencil lines show.
4. Using a single-knotted basting thread, baste with running stitches around the folded edges of the fabric. (I like to use quilting thread because it is strong and will pull out later without breaking.) Keep the knot on the right side of the fabric so that the basting thread is easy to remove after the appliqué is complete.

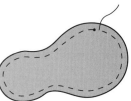

Wrong Side   Right Side

Clip curves to fold if necessary.   No need to knot end.

5. Pin or baste appliqué pieces to the background fabric. I baste only if the appliqué is large or irregular in shape.

6. Using a small, very thin needle (called a sharp) and a single, matching thread with one end knotted, blindstitch the appliqué piece to the background as shown below.

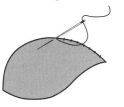

Blind stitch

Hand Appliqué – Method 2 – Freezer Paper

While this method can be time-consuming and cumbersome, I find it to be the best method for appliquéing small, perfect circles, leaves, or any small piece that is repeated numerous times and is expected to look exactly the same.

There are several variations of the freezer-paper method. I use the following.

1. Trace the reverse of each pattern piece onto the uncoated side of the freezer paper. (For circles and most leaves, the reverse would be the same.)

2. Cut out the pieces of paper on the marked line. Press the paper pieces with coated side down to the wrong side of the appropriate fabrics. Cut fabrics ¼" larger than the paper pattern all around.

3. Pin the pieces in place as you appliqué and use the needle to turn the raw edges under. The freezer paper works as a stabilizer and helps you achieve neat, rounded edges.

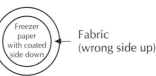

Press paper to fabric.

4. Appliqué pieces using a blind stitch. When the appliqué is complete, slit the background fabric behind the appliquéd piece and remove the freezer paper. If the paper piece is large and well adhered to the fabric, use a manicurist's orange stick to loosen it and tweezers to pull it out through the slit fabric.

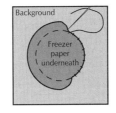

Use the needle to push raw edges under freezer paper.

Hand Appliqué – Method 3 – Paper Patch

One of the oldest methods used to get nice, smooth-edged circles is the paper-patch method. This method works well for circles, but does not work at all for irregular shapes or any piece with a concave curve.

1. Trace the pattern pieces onto heavy bond paper and cut them out. Cut fabric piece ¼" larger than patterns.

2. With a single, knotted thread, sew a running stitch around the edges of the fabric piece.

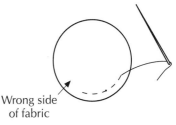

Wrong side of fabric

3. Place the paper pattern next to the wrong side of the fabric piece. Pull stitches taut around paper.

4. Knot end and press with paper inside.

5. Remove the paper and proceed to appliqué. Or appliqué first and then slit the background fabric to remove the paper when the appliqué is complete. Use tweezers to remove paper.

Hand Appliqué – Method 4 – Stitch and Turn

This method is helpful for those who suffer from arthritis or who feel "all thumbs" when it comes to appliqué. It is also useful for small, irregularly shaped pieces.

1. Mark patterns and fabrics as in the basted method, with one exception: mark fabrics on the wrong side and omit the embroidery lines until later. Cut pieces ¼" larger than pattern lines indicate.

2. Use a nonfusible, lightweight interfacing to back the fabric pieces. Cut the interfacing slightly larger than the fabric pieces. Place the right side of the fabric against the interfacing and machine stitch around the piece on the marked line.

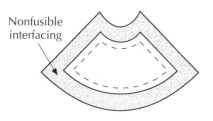

Nonfusible interfacing

Trim the interfacing to match the fabric, clipping curves if necessary.

3. Cut a small slash in the center of the interfacing and turn the piece right side out. Use a manicurist's orange stick to help turn it, if necessary. Press. Using a light table and marking tool of your choice, mark the embroidery lines. Appliqué the piece to the background using a blind stitch.

❧ *Embroidery*

Always use a good-quality embroidery floss and small embroidery needles. I often use a size 10 quilting needle. The smaller the needle, the finer the stitch you will achieve.

If you are using pearl cotton for embroidery, as suggested for "The Three Little Kittens" on page 31, you will need a larger needle with a larger eye.

A good embroidery hoop to hold the fabric taut is a must. I prefer the plastic type with metal spring used for machine embroidery.

Use two strands of floss (never three) for most embroidery. For small details, or for dates and signatures, I use just one strand. For example, on the lips in "Guardian Angel" on page 52, I used one strand in order to get a neater, more delicate line.

Although there are entire books filled with the various embroidery stitches, I have included only those necessary for the patterns in this book.

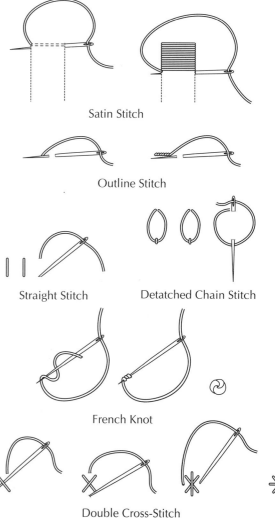

Satin Stitch

Outline Stitch

Straight Stitch

Detatched Chain Stitch

French Knot

Double Cross-Stitch

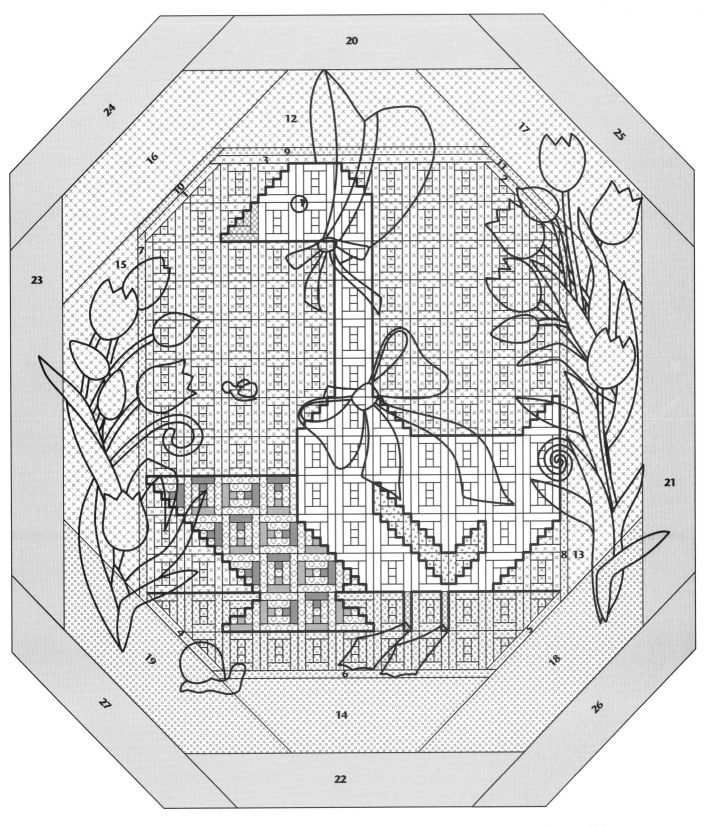

Photo: page 41• Size: 46″ x 51½″ • 139 Blocks • Finished Block Size: 2¹/₂″ x 2¹/₂″

Traditional Blocks

Make 7.
White, aquas
Goose/Sky

Make 6.
White, gray
Goose wing

Make 1.
Orange, aquas
Beak

Make 1.
White, tan and
brown #1
Goose/Basket

Make 1.
White, tan and
aquas
Goose/Basket

Unusual Blocks

Make 3.
Tan, aquas and brown #2
Basket/Sky

For pieces 1, 2, 3, 4 and 11,
cut 1" squares. For piece 10,
cut a 1" x 2½" strip.
Sew 1 to 2, 3 to 4, 10 to 11.
Sew unit 1/2 to unit 3/4 and
continue piecing in order,
finishing with unit 10/11.

Make 1.
Greens, tan and brown #1
Basket/Grass

For pieces 1, 2, 3, 4 and 8,
cut 1" squares. For piece 9,
cut a 1" x 2" strip.
Sew 1 to 2, 3 to 4, 8 to 9.
Sew unit 1/2 to unit 3/4 and
continue piecing in order.

Courthouse Steps Blocks

Make 68.
Aquas
Sky

Make 25.
White
Goose

Make 14.
Greens
Grass

Make 9.
Tan, brown #1
and brown #2
Basket

Make 2.
Greens, orange
Grass/Legs

Make 1.
Greens, tans
and brown #1
Basket/Grass

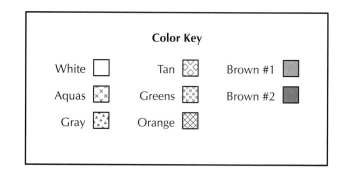

Color Key

White	Tan	Brown #1
Aquas	Greens	Brown #2
Gray	Orange	

Materials: 44"- wide fabric

1⅛ yds. total assorted aquas for sky

¾ yd. extra of one of the aquas for border

1 yd. total assorted greens for grass and leaves

⅝ yd. extra of one of the grass greens for the border

½ yd. white for goose

⅓ yd. yellow floral print for bonnet and bow

¼ yd. tan for basket

⅛ yd. brown #1 for basket

⅛ yd. brown #2 for basket

⅛ yd. gray for goose's wing

⅛ yd. dark pink #1 for bonnet lining, bow lining, and tulips

⅛ yd. dark pink #2 for bonnet, bow, and tulips

⅛ yd. orange for goose's bill and feet, tulips, bee, and snail

1 yd. light green print for border

3¼ yds. dark green for binding and backing

Scraps of the following fabrics:

    Black for eye

    Yellow for tulips, bee, and snail

    Light pink for tulips

Notions: black, orange, dark pink, gold, white, and green embroidery floss; extra-wide tan bias tape for basket handle; regular-width green bias tape for stems

Directions

1. Color in the quilt plan and blocks with colored pencils to help eliminate mistakes.

2. Make a sample block to test the accuracy of your seam allowance. The block should measure 3" square (2½" square when sewn into the quilt.)

3. Before making the blocks, be sure to reserve enough of the greens for leaves, and pinks and oranges for tulips.

4. Using either the speed-piecing method or templates, make blocks shown on page 22.

5. When all the blocks are completed, sew the blocks together in horizontal rows as shown in the quilt plan on page 21. Sew the rows together, making sure to match the seams between each block. Trim off excess sections of blocks as shown on quilt plan.

6. Use extra aqua and green strips to make borders 1–6.

7. Cut the following strips for borders.

    From the darkest green, cut:

      1 strip, 1" x 20"

      2 strips, 1" x 10"

      2 strips, 1" x 27"

    From the green border fabric, cut:

      1 strip, 1" x 20"

      2 strips, 1" x 10"

      1 strip, 5½" x 20"

      2 strips, 5½" x 23"

    From the aqua border fabric, cut:

      1 strip, 5½" x 20"

      2 strips, 5½" x 29"

      2 strips, 5½" x 23"

    From the light green print for border, cut:

      2 strips, 4" x 33"

      2 strips, 4" x 25"

      4 strips, 4" x 23"

8. Add the borders, one at a time, following the numerical order on the quilt plan on page 21. Trim excess fabric as you go.

With right sides together, sew strips 1 and 2 to quilt top along edge, using ¼" seam allowances.

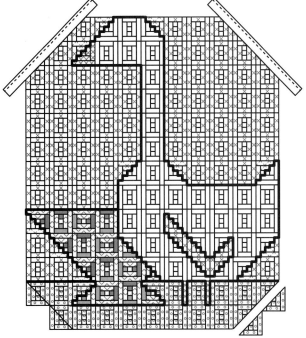

Trim blocks at all four corners.

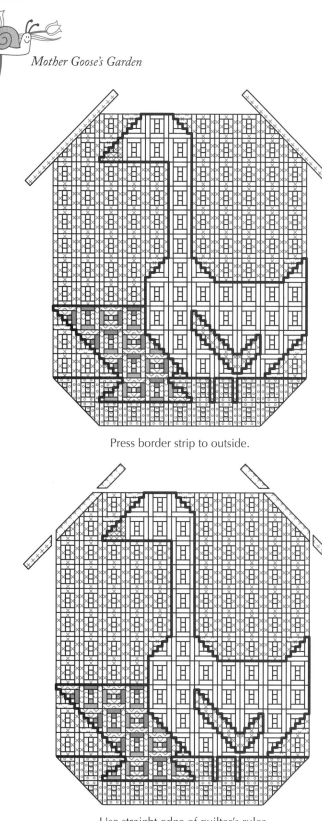

Press border strip to outside.

Use straight edge of quilter's ruler
and rotary cutter to trim excess.

9. Using the templates (T-1 on the pullout patterns), complete the appliqué in the following order:

>*handle* to basket (use tan bias tape; arch the handle, to make it appear to go behind goose's neck.)

>*neckband and bow* to goose's neck
>*inner bonnet, bonnet, and ribbon* to goose's head
>*eye* to goose
>*stems* to background (use green bias tape)
>*tendrils, stems, leaves, then tulips* to quilt
>*feet* to goose
>*bee* to sky
>*snail* to grass

10. Complete the embroidery. See page 20 for embroidery stitches.

>*goose's eyelashes*—black outline stitch
>*"gleams" in goose's and bee's eyes*—white satin stitch
>*inner tulip lines*—pink, gold, or orange outline stitch
>*leaf veins*—green outline stitch
>*tendril details*—green double cross-stitch
>*bee's stripes, hair, mouth, and antennae*—black outline stitch
>*bee's eyes and antennae tips*—black satin stitch
>*snail's mouth and antennae*—black outline stitch
>*snail's eyes and antennae tips*—black satin stitch
>*snail's shell curl*—orange outline stitch

11. Mark the top for quilting. Mark vertical lines in the grass area, cross-hatch grid lines in the basket ½" apart, feathers on the goose, and lines radiating from the goose in the aqua border. Draw a diagonal cross-hatch grid in the green-print border 1" apart.

12. Layer quilt top, batting, and backing. Pin or baste layers together. Quilt on all marked lines and around leaves, tulips, bee, snail, goose, goose wing, bow, and bonnet. Quilt in-the-ditch along the inner green border.

13. When quilting is complete, trim batting and backing to match quilt top. Bind edges with 2½"-wide strips of fabric, using the regular binding method on pages 86–87, with one variation. Sew the strips to the quilt top, stitching 1" (rather than the normal ¼") from the quilt edge. This makes a wider binding.

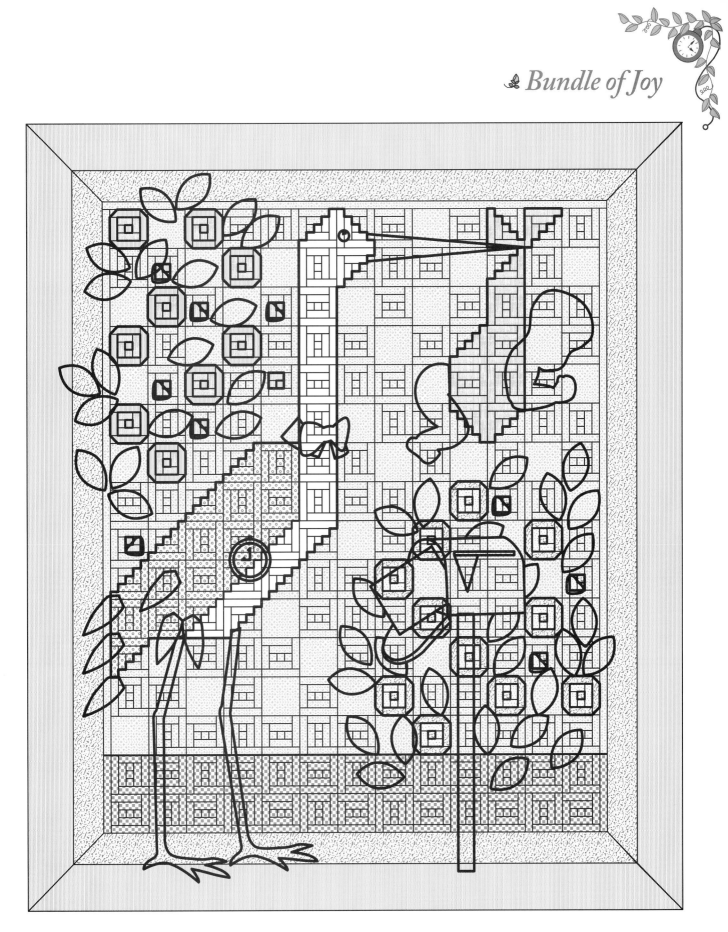

Photo: page 42 • Size: 42″ x 49″ • 208 Blocks • Finished Block Size: 2½″ x 2½″

Traditional Blocks

   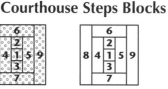

Make 7.
Aquas, light
purples and
dark purples
Buds

Make 6.
Whites and
aquas
Stork/
Background

Make 6.
Light purples
and aquas
Bundle/
Background

Make 5.
Grays and
aquas
Stork/
Background

Make 3.
Whites and
grays
Stork

Make 3.
Aquas, dk. and
lt. peaches
Buds

Courthouse Steps Blocks

Make 74.
Aquas
Background

Make 26.
Greens
Grass

Make 9.
Grays
Stork

Make 7.
Whites
Stork

Make 4.
Light purples
Bundle

Make 38.
Aquas
Background

Unusual Blocks

The following blocks are "rounded" Traditional blocks.
Begin by making normal Traditional blocks and then
"rounding" the corners. See page 11.

Make 11.
Light peaches,
dark peaches
and aquas
Roses

Make 9.
Light purples,
dark purples
and aquas
Roses

Color Key

Aquas	Grays	Greens
Lt. purples	Lt. peaches	White
Dk. purples	Dk. peaches	

Materials: 44"- wide fabric

1½ yds. total assorted aquas for background

½ yd. total assorted shades of peach for roses,
stork legs and bill, mailbox flag, and stork's
bow tie

½ yd. total assorted medium greens for grass

½ yd. total assorted grays for stork wing and
mailbox

⅓ yd. total assorted purples for roses, baby
bundle, and stork collar

¼ yd. total assorted whites for stork, letter, and
watch

¼ yd. skin-tone fabric for baby

⅛ yd. brown for mailbox post

⅔ yd. purple for border

⅓ yd. peach for border

2 yds. for binding and backing
  Scraps of the following fabrics:
    Dark greens for leaves and buds
    Dark brown for stork eye and mailbox
      flag pole
    Gold for watch
    Dark gray for inner mailbox

Notions: white, dark brown, dark green and black embroidery floss*; ⅓ yd. peach ribbon for baby's hair bow; fabric paint or crayon for cheeks

A black fine-tip permanent marking pen can be used instead of embroidery floss for writing details on letter.

Directions

1. Color in the quilt plan and blocks with colored pencils to help eliminate mistakes.

2. Make a sample block to test the accuracy of your seam allowance. The block should measure 3" square (it will be 2½" square when sewn into the quilt).

3. Before making the blocks, be sure to reserve enough of each fabric needed for the appliqué pieces.

4. Using either the speed-piecing method or templates, make the blocks shown on page 26.

5. When all the blocks are completed, sew the blocks together in vertical rows as shown in the quilt plan on page 25. Sew the rows together, making sure to match the seams between each block.

6. For the border sections, cut:
   2 aqua strips, 1" x 35½"
   1 aqua strip, 1" x 34"
   2 green strips, 1" x 5½"
   2 peach strips, 2" x 43"
   2 peach strips, 2" x 50" (piece for length if needed)
   2 purple strips, 3" x 43"
   2 purple strips, 3" x 50" (piece for length if needed)

7. Sew each green strip to a 1" x 35½" aqua strip, and attach one pieced strip to each side of the quilt. Sew the 1" x 34" aqua strip to the top. Sew each peach strip to a matching purple strip to make 4 border sections. Attach border strips to each side of the quilt and miter corners as shown on pages 84–85.

8. Using the templates (T-2 on the pullout patterns), complete the appliqué:
   leaves to background (leaves and bud shanks shown in the photo on page 42 are machine appliquéd with a satin stitch)
   green to buds
   baby to bundle
   post, mailbox, and letter to background (over leaves and roses)
   flag to mailbox
   collar, then bow, to stork
   watch, bill, eye, legs, then feathers, to stork

9. Complete the embroidery. See page 20 for embroidery stitches.
   baby's hair, lashes, ear, fingers, toes, and skin creases—dark brown outline stitch
   line in stork's bill—dark brown outline stitch
   watch hands—dark brown outline stitch
   watch chain—chain stitch
   ends of watch chain—satin stitch
   numbers on watch—straight stitch
   bow tie—dark brown outline stitch
   leaf veins—dark green outline stitch or machine embroidered satin stitch
   "gleam" in stork's eye—white satin stitch
   writing on letter—single strand of black outline stitch (or use permanent marking pen)

10. Mark the top for quilting. Draw vertical zigzags in the grass area, wavy lines in the sky, feathers on the stork, and spirals on the roses. Mark scallops in the border.

11. Layer quilt top, batting, and backing. Pin or baste layers together. Quilt on marked lines and around all leaves, roses, stork, watch, bow tie, baby, bundle, mailbox, and letter. Tie bow and sew to baby's curl.

12. Trim batting and backing to match quilt top. Bind edges with 2½"-wide strips of fabric, using the double-fold method on pages 87–88.

Humpty Dumpty

Photo: page 43 • Size: 43½" x 56" • 266 Blocks • Finished Block Size: 2½" x 2½"

Traditional Blocks

Make 8. Tans and off-white Egg/Collar	Make 4. Tans and dk. blues Egg/Sky	Make 2. Off-white and green Collar/Grass	Make 1. Off-white and dk. reds Collar/Brick

Make 1. Green and dk. blues Grass/Sky	Make 1. Off-white and med. reds Collar/Brick	Make 1. Dk. reds and med. reds Top brick	Make 1. Med. blues, dk. blues and gold Soldier's cuff

Courthouse Steps Blocks

Make 37. Dk. blues Sky	Make 37. Med. reds Bricks	Make 36. Dk. reds Bricks	Make 35. Lt. reds Bricks

Make 12. Med. blues and gold Soldier's buttons	Make 6. Med. blues and dk. blue Soldier's jacket	Make 4. Off-white Collar	Make 2. Black Soldier's shoes

Unusual Blocks

Make 2. Med. blues and gold Soldier's epaulets	Make 1. Med. blues, dk. blues and gold Soldier's cuff

Make 32. Tans Egg/Castle	Make 26. Green Grass	Make 12. Dk. blues and gold Soldier's pants	Make 2. Lt. brown Castle

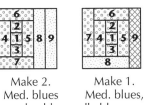

Make 2. Med. blues Soldier's jacket	Make 1. Burgundies Top brick

Color Key

Tans ▫	Green ▦	Dk. reds ▨	Lt. browns ▨
Med. blues ▨	Lt. reds ▵	Golds ▫	Burgundies ▦
Dk. blues ▨	Med. reds ▨	Black ■	Off-white ▫

Materials: 44"- wide fabric

1 yd. total assorted dark blues for sky, pants, bow tie, and flag

²⁄₃ yd. total assorted medium reds for bricks, feather, flags, and soldier's sash

⁵⁄₈ yd. total assorted light reds for bricks

⁵⁄₈ yd. total assorted dark reds for bricks

⁵⁄₈ yd. total assorted tans for Humpty Dumpty and castle

³⁄₈ yd. total assorted medium blues for soldier's jacket and plume

½ yd. dark green for grass

⅓ yd. off-white for collar and soldier's gloves

⅓ yd. medium gold for road, castle turrets, and Humpty's legs and hat

⅛ yd. dark gold for Humpty's hat and gloves and soldier's buttons, cuffs, and epaulets

¾ yd. tan for border

3 yds. for binding and backing

Scraps of the following fabrics:
Assorted greens for leaves
Black for soldier's shoes
Light peach for Humpty's cheeks and soldier's face
Dark peach for Humpty's lips and cheek shadow
Light brown for Humpty's boots and castle
Burgundy for brick

Notions: black, white, peach, and gold embroidery floss; black, green, and red bias tape for flagpole, vine, and brick wall

Directions

1. Color in the quilt plan and blocks with colored pencils to help eliminate mistakes.
2. Make a sample block to test the accuracy of your seam allowance. The block should measure 3" square (it will be 2½" square when sewn into the quilt.)
3. Before making the blocks, be sure to reserve enough of each fabric for the appliqué pieces.
4. Using either the speed-piecing method or templates, make blocks shown on page 29.
5. When all the blocks are completed, sew the blocks together in horizontal rows as shown in the quilt plan on page 28. Then sew the rows together, making sure to match the seams between each block.
6. For borders, cut:
   - 2 strips of tan, 4" x 44", for inner border
   - 2 strips of tan, 4" x 57" (piece for length), for inner border
   - Cut random lengths of leftover 1"-wide red strips from brick fabrics and sew together to make:
   - 2 strips of assorted reds, 1" x 44", for outer border
   - 2 strips of assorted reds, 1" x 57", for outer border
7. Sew each red strip to a matching tan strip to make 4 border sections. Attach border sections to each side of the quilt and miter corners as shown on pages 84–85.
8. Using the templates (T-3 on the pullout patterns), complete the appliqué:
   - *red bias tape* between first and second row of bricks
   - *hat, feather, hatband and hat button* to Humpty's head
   - *eyes, lips, cheeks, and cheek shadow* to Humpty's face
   - *bow* to Humpty's collar
   - *arms, then gloves* to Humpty's side
   - *bias-tape vines, then leaves*
   - *legs, then boots* to Humpty
   - *hat, face, eyes, cheeks, plume, and button* to soldier
   - *gloves, sash, and shoe tips* to soldier
   - *bias-tape flagpole and flags*
   - *door, flag, and turrets* to castle
   - *road* to grass
9. Complete the embroidery. See page 20 for embroidery stitches.
   - *Humpty's nose, mouth, eyebrows, and fingers*—black outline stitch
   - *feather lines*—black outline stitch
   - *soldier's nose, mouth, eyebrows, and thumbs*—black outline stitch
   - *leaf veins and castle windows*—black outline stitch
   - *lines in bow tie*—white outline stitch
   - *boot tassels*—gold outline stitch
   - *"gleam" in eyes*—white satin stitch
   - *shine on soldier's cheeks and bottom lip*—peach satin stitch
10. Mark the top for quilting. Draw clouds in the sky and horizontal waves in the grass. Mark the border with a design of your choice.
11. Layer quilt top, batting, and backing. Pin or baste layers together. Quilt on marked lines and around each brick, leaf, and detail of Humpty and soldier. Quilt around castle, flags, and road.
12. When quilting is complete, trim batting and backing to match quilt top. Bind edges with 2½"-wide strips of fabric, using the double-fold method on pages 87–88.

Photo: page 44 • Size: 67″ x 77¹⁄₂″ • 304 Blocks • Finished Block Size: 3¹⁄₂″ x 3¹⁄₂″

The Three Little Kittens

Traditional Blocks

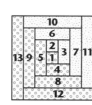

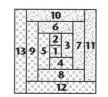

Make 8.
Dk. aqua #1 and
med. aquas
Mittens

Make 8.
Pink #1 and
med. aquas
Mittens

Make 4.
Med. aquas
and whites
Kitten

Make 4.
Med. aquas and
med. golds
Kitten

Make 4.
Med. aquas
and peaches
Kitten

Make 4.
White print and
med. aquas
Mittens

Make 2.
Med. aquas,
golds and
white print
Mitten

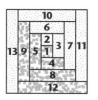

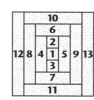
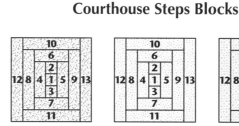
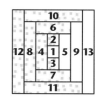

Make 2.
Golds and dk.
gold
Kitten

Make 1.
Dk. pink and
med. golds
Kitten's ear

Make 1.
Dk. pink and
whites
Kitten's ear

Make 1.
Dk. pink and
peaches
Kitten's ear

Courthouse Steps Blocks

Make 93.
Med. aquas
Background

Make 22.
Whites
Kitten/Mitten

Make 20.
Peaches
Kitten

Make 14.
Med. golds
Kitten

Make 12.
White print and
med. golds
Mitten

Make 8.
Pink #1 and
whites
Mitten

Make 6.
Dk. aqua #1
Mittens

Make 6.
Med. rust and
dk. aqua #1
Mittens

Make 4.
Med. rust and
dk. aqua #1
Mittens

Make 4.
White print
Mittens

Make 4.
Med. golds
and dk. golds
Kitten

Make 4.
Pink #1 and
whites
Mittens

Make 2.
Pink #1
Mittens

Make 2.
Dk. pink and
white
Kitten's ears

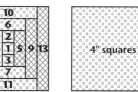

Make 2.
Dk. pink and
peach
Kitten's ears

Make 2.
Dk. pink and
med. gold
Kitten's ears

Make 2.
Med. aquas
and pink #1
Mittens

Make 2.
Med. aquas
and white
print
Mittens

Make 2.
Med. aquas and
dk. aqua #1
Mittens

Cut 43.
Med. aqua
Background

Unusual Blocks

  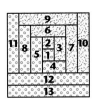 

| Make 2.
Med. aquas,
white print and
med. golds
Mittens | Make 1.
Dk. pink and
peaches
Kitten's ear | Make 1.
Med. aquas
and whites
Kitten's chin | Make 1.
Med. aquas
and peaches
Kitten's chin | Make 1.
Med. aquas
and peaches
Kitten's chin | Make 1.
Med. aquas
and golds
Kitten's chin | Make 1.
Med. aquas
and golds
Kitten's chin |

| Make 1.
Med. aquas
and whites
Kitten's chin | Make 1.
Dk. pink and
golds
Kitten's ear | Make 1.
Dk. pink and
whites
Kitten's ear |

Color Key

Whites ☐	Dk. aqua #1 ⊠	Med. golds ▦	Med. rust ▦
White print ▦	Pink #1 ☐	Dk. golds ▦	
Med. aquas ▦	Dk. pink ▦	Peaches ▦	

Materials: 44"- wide fabric

3½ yds. total assorted medium aquas for background

2¼ yds. aqua print or polka dot for border and background squares

½ yd. dark aqua #1 for mittens and kitten's eyes

⅛ yd. dark aqua #2 for eyes, tears, and hearts

1 yd. total assorted whites for kitten and pink mitten

⅝ yd. white print for mittens

⅞ yd. total assorted medium golds for kitten and mitten

⅛ yd. dark gold for stripes on kitten

1 yd. total assorted peaches for kitten and bow

½ yd. pink print #1 for mittens

⅛ yd. pink print #2 for bow

⅓ yd. dark pink for inner ears

¼ yd. medium rust for mittens

4½ yds. for binding and backing

Scraps of the following fabrics:
Dark rust for noses
Black for eyes
Yellow for bow
Dark peach for inner peach bow

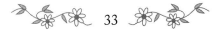

Notions: black pearl cotton; white embroidery floss

Directions

1. Color in the quilt plan and blocks with colored pencils to help eliminate mistakes.
2. Make a sample block to test the accuracy of your seam allowance. The block should measure 4" square (it will be 3½" square when sewn into the quilt.)
3. Before cutting fabric for blocks, reserve enough of each fabric needed for appliqué pieces (T-4 on the pullout patterns). Also reserve a 24" x 2¼ yard piece of the aqua border fabric for border strips.
4. Using either the speed-piecing method or templates, make the blocks shown on pages 32–33.
5. When all the blocks are completed, sew the blocks together in horizontal rows as shown in the quilt plan on page 31. Sew the rows together, making sure to match the seams between each block.
6. Cut the reserved aqua border fabric into four 6"-wide strips: cut 2 of the strips 80" long for the quilt sides, and cut 2 of the strips 70" long for the top and bottom of the quilt.
7. Attach border strips to each side of the quilt and miter corners as shown on pages 84–85.
8. Using the templates (T-4 on the pullout patterns), complete the appliqué:
   eyes to peach and gold kittens
   noses to all kittens
   tears to white kitten
   tongue to gold kitten
   bows to background
   dots to aqua mittens
   hearts to white mittens
   flowers to pink mittens

9. Complete the embroidery. See page 20 for embroidery stitches.
   white kitten's eyelashes and mouth—black outline stitch
   shine on tears—white satin stitch
   peach kitten's mouth—black outline stitch
   gold kitten's mouth and tongue—black outline stitch
   wrinkles in bows—black outline stitch
10. Mark the top for quilting. Draw whiskers and eyebrows on kittens. Mark evenly spaced cross-hatch grid lines in the background blocks and scallops on borders.
11. Layer quilt top, batting, and backing. Baste or pin layers together. Quilt on marked lines and around kittens' eyes, noses, mouths, heads, bow, and mittens. Quilt in-the-ditch around all designs in mittens.
12. When quilting is complete, cut all 3 layers of scalloped border ½" outside the last row of quilting. Bind edges using 1½"-wide bias strips and the regular binding method on pages 86–87.

Photo: page 45 • Size: 45″ x 38″ • 80 Blocks • Finished Block Size: 3¹/₂″ x 3¹/₂″

Courageous Lion

Traditional Blocks

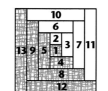 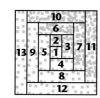

Make 5.
Golds and rust
Mane/Face

Make 3.
Rust and beiges
Mane/Background

Make 3.
Golds and beiges
Lion/Background

Make 2.
Dk. brown and
beiges
Lion/Background

Make 1.
Golds and
dk. brown
Lion

Make 1.
Golds, beiges
and dk. brown
Lion

Courthouse Steps Blocks

Make 20.
Golds
Lion

Make 15.
Beiges
Background

Make 9.
Rust and beiges
Mane/Background

Make 3.
Rust and golds
Mane/Body

Make 2.
Dk. brown
Lion

Make 2.
Beiges and
dk. brown
Feet

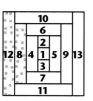

Make 1.
Beiges and
golds
Foot

Make 1.
Dk. brown
and golds
Foot

4" Squares

Cut 12.
Beiges
Background

Color Key

Beiges ☐   Dk. brown ▨

Golds ▦   Rust ▨

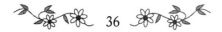

Materials: 44"- wide fabric

1yd. assorted beiges for background

1 yd. total assorted golds for body

½ yd. rust for mane and tail

¼ yd. dark brown for body, nose, and eyes

¼ yd. total greens and browns for leaves

1⅓ yds. border print with 4 repeats in the
    design for border. (1⅓ yds. of any
    fabric may be used instead of a
    border print)

2½ yds. for binding and backing

Scraps of the following fabrics:
    Light gold for nose, ears, and eyelids
    Yellow for eyes
    Solid black for eyes
    Dark rust for inner ears
    Red, pink, and burgundy for berries

Notions: Black and white embroidery floss

Directions

1. Color in the quilt plan and blocks with colored pencils to help eliminate mistakes.

2. Make a sample block to test the accuracy of your seam allowance. The block should measure 4" square (it will be 3½" square when sewn into the quilt.)

3. Before cutting fabric for blocks, be sure to reserve a piece of gold for the tail, and rust for the tail tip. Also, reserve some of each beige background to cut a total of twelve 4" squares.

4. Using either the speed-piecing method or templates, make the blocks shown on page 36.

5. When all the blocks are completed, sew the blocks together in horizontal rows as shown in the quilt plan on page 35. Sew the rows together, making sure to match the seams between each block.

6. Cut the border print into 4 repeat border strips. The length will be determined by the width of the border strips. If you are not using a border print fabric, cut 4 strips from the lengthwise grain, 5" x 46". Attach border strips to each side of the quilt and miter corners as shown on pages 84–85.

7. Using the templates (T-5 on the pullout patterns), complete the appliqué:
    eyes, nose, and ears to face
    berries in clusters
    leaves
    tail to body

8. Complete the embroidery. See page 20 for embroidery stitches.
    berry stems—black outline stitch, 2 rows
    lion's smile—black outline stitch, 2 rows
    eyelashes—black outline stitch
    "gleam" in eyes—white satin stitch
    claws—black outline stitch

9. Mark the quilt top for quilting. Draw veins in leaves and shaggy lines in mane. Mark the background and border as desired.

10. Layer quilt top, batting, and backing. Pin or baste layers together. Quilt on marked lines and around lion, face, eyes, nose, ears, leaves, and berries.

11. When quilting is complete, trim batting and backing to match quilt top. Bind edges with 2½"-wide strips of fabric, using the double-fold binding method on pages 87–88.

Terrific Tiger

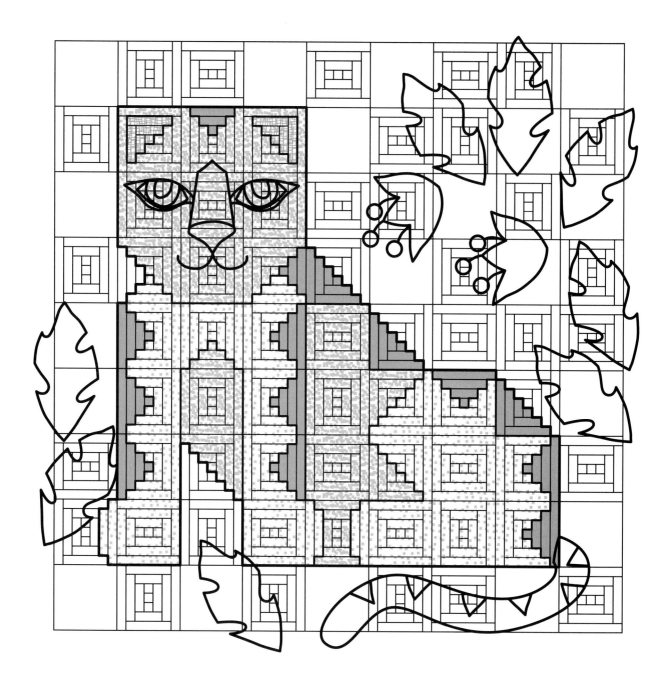

Photo: page 46 • Size: 37″ x 37″ • 81 Blocks • Finished Block Size: 3½″x 3½″

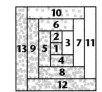

Traditional Blocks

Make 3.	Make 2.	Make 2.	Make 1.	Make 1.	Make 1.
Beiges and black Stripes/ Background	Med. golds and dk. golds Tiger	Dk. golds and rust Ears	Dk. golds and beiges Tiger/ Background	Dk. golds, med. golds and beiges Head/Shoulder	Dk. golds, black and med. golds Head/Shoulder

Courthouse Steps Blocks

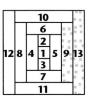

Make 26.	Make 9.	Make 8.	Make 5.	Make 1.	Make 1.
Beiges Background	Med. golds and black Tiger stripes	Dk. golds Tiger	Med. golds Tiger	Med. golds and dk. golds Chest	Dk. golds and black Head

Make 1.	Make 1.	Cut 19.
Beiges and med. golds Foot	Dk. golds and med. golds Feet	Beiges Background

4" Squares

Color Key

Beiges		Dk. golds	
Med. golds		Rust	
Black			

Terrific Tiger

Materials: 44"- wide fabric

1¼ yds. total assorted beiges for background
¾ yd. total assorted medium golds for body, nose, eyes, tail, and flower
½ yd. total assorted dark golds for head and body
¼ yd. black for tiger stripes
¼ yd. rust for inner border, ears, and flowers
¼ yd. total greens and browns for leaves
⅓ yd. tiger print for outer border
1⅞ yds. for binding and backing
Scraps of the following fabrics:
    Black solid for eyes and nose
    Dark rust for flowers

Notions: Black and white embroidery floss

Directions

1. Color in the quilt plan and blocks with colored pencils to help eliminate mistakes.
2. Make a sample block to test the accuracy of your seam allowance. The block should measure 4" square (it will be 3½" square when sewn into the quilt.)
3. Before cutting strips for blocks, be sure to reserve enough gold for eyes, nose, flower, and tail. Also, reserve some of each beige to cut a total of nineteen 4" squares.
4. Using either the speed-piecing method or templates, make blocks shown on page 39.
5. When all the blocks are completed, sew the blocks together in vertical rows as shown in the quilt plan on page 38. Then sew the rows together, making sure to match the seams between each block.

6. For the border sections, cut:
    four 1" x 38" rust strips
    four 2½" x 38" tiger print strips
    Sew a rust strip to a tiger print strip. Repeat 3 times for a total of 4 border sections. Attach border strips to each side of the quilt and miter corners as shown on pages 84–85.
7. Using the templates (T-5 on the pullout patterns), complete the appliqué:
    eyes and nose to face
    stripes to tail
    tail to body
    flowers and leaves to background
8. Complete the embroidery. See page 20 for embroidery stitches.
    flower petals and stems—black outline stitch
    mouth—black outline stitch, 2 rows
    eyelashes—black outline stitch
    "gleam" in eyes—white satin stitch
    claws—black outline stitch
9. Mark the top for quilting, drawing veins in the leaves. Mark the background and border as desired.
10. Layer quilt top, batting, and backing. Pin or baste layers together. Quilt on marked lines and around tiger, tiger stripes, eyes, nose, leaves, and flowers.
11. When quilting is complete, trim batting and backing to match quilt top. Bind edges with 2½"-wide strips of fabric, using the double-fold method on pages 87–88.

Gallery

"Mother Goose's Garden," 1987, designed by Carin Christerson and Christal Carter, Valley Center, California, 46" x 51½". Pieced, appliquéd, and quilted by Christal Carter.

My daughter Carin designed a Log Cabin goose and basket on graph paper when she was still in high school. I thought the design would make a wonderful "Mother Goose," so I added a bonnet and bow, along with a snail, honey bee, and some tulips. This wonderful little crib quilt will someday belong to Carin's first child.

"Bundle of Joy," 1993, by Christal Carter, Valley Center, California, 42" x 49".

A book of children's quilts would not be complete without Mr. Stork delivering his "Bundle of Joy." The letter in the mailbox announces the baby's name, address, birth date, and weight. Mr. Stork's pocket watch tells the time of birth.

"Humpty Dumpty," 1993, designed by Christal Carter, Valley Center, California, 43½" x 56".
Pieced and appliquéd by Christal Carter; machine quilted by Barbara Ford.

For a special gift, present this quilt to a beloved child along with a book of nursery rhymes to inspire a love of books. Humpty Dumpty sits on a wall while one of the King's men stands guard nearby.

"The Three Little Kittens," 1993, by Christal Carter, Valley Center, California, 67" x 77½".

Inspired by the nursery rhyme about the kittens who lost their mittens, this quilt is sure to charm any cat lover or child. While these colors depict our own Snow Puddin', Pumpkin, and Sasha, you can easily change the color scheme to portray your own kittens.

"Courageous Lion," 1993, by Christal Carter, Valley Center, California, 45" x 38". Pieced and appliquéd by Christal Carter; machine quilted by Barbara Ford.

Lions and Tigers and Bears! Oh My! The following trio of quilts was originally designed as one large quilt. But because larger quilts sometimes seem overwhelming to quiltmakers, I decided to break the design down into a series of three small quilts. Adventurous quilters can place the three whimsical beasts in one large design.

Courageous Lion

This friendly beast would be happy on the wall of any child's room. To adapt to a crib quilt or larger lap quilt, add borders with the child's name and birth date to the top and bottom of the quilt. You could use the Alphabet blocks included with the "Toytime Teddy" quilt instructions, which begin on page 56.

Gallery

"Terrific Tiger," 1993, by Christal Carter, Valley Center, California, 37" x 37". Pieced and appliquéd by Christal Carter; machine quilted by Barbara Ford.

Terrific Tiger

This is the second quilt in the animal series. Shown sitting among the jungle flowers, this tiger would make a g-r-reat birthday gift. He could also be made as a wall quilt or as the center section of a twin-size quilt.

"Honey Bear," 1993, by Christal Carter, Valley Center, California, 36" x 43". Pieced and appliquéd by Christal Carter; machine quilted by Barbara Ford.

Honey Bear

"Honey Bear" is the last design in the "Lions and Tigers and Bears" series. What little child would not like to snuggle up with this delightful animal? He happily picks wild flowers and smiles at a nearby honeybee.

"Toytime Teddy," 1986, by Christal Carter, Valley Center, California, 82" x 92".

Although I designed and made this large quilt many years ago, I never put it into pattern form until now. The happy Teddy sits with his toy car and block, and holds a bouquet of balloons. He is bordered by the alphabet and numbers, with toys in the four quilt corners (boat, drum, top, and kite). The quilt belongs to my youngest daughter, Catrina, who collects bears. The C, T, and B on the block stand for "Catrina's Teddy Bear." Personalize "Toytime Teddy" with your child's initials.

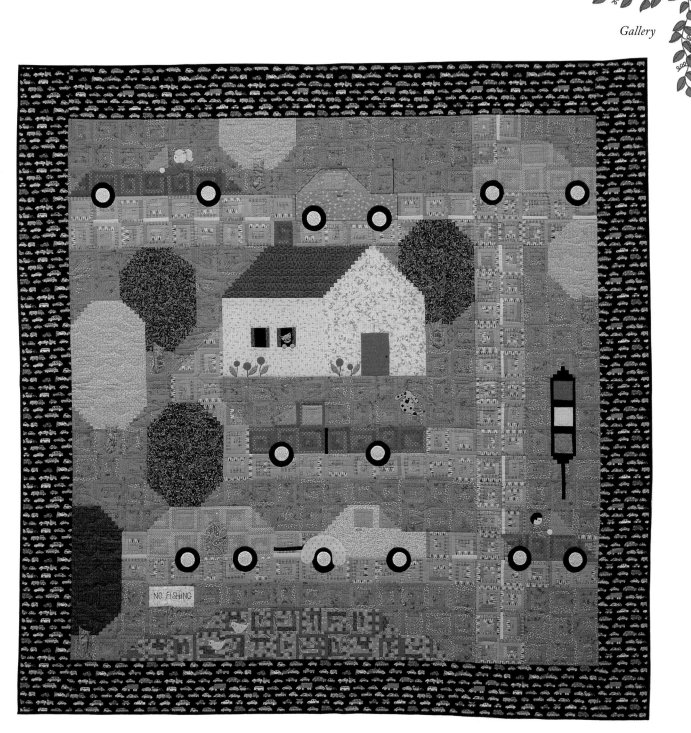

"Stop and Go," 1993, by Christal Carter, Valley Center, California, 87½" x 87½". Pieced and appliquéd by Christal Carter; machine quilted by Barbara Ford.

This busy scene is sure to delight any child who enjoys toy cars. Sports cars, sedans, a truck, and even a travel trailer are included in this large quilt. Bright colors echo the colors of a traffic light and work well to illustrate the fruit trees, house, and pond. Personalize the quilt by adding the child's address, the family car, and, of course, the child himself!

"The Old Oak Tree," 1990, Christal Carter, Valley Center, California, 44½" x 47".

I designed this quilt as a symbol of homecoming. Personalize the design by adding animals, children, or whatever is meaningful to the recipient of the quilt. One of my students added her five children and three dogs. She even appliquéd oranges to the tree because she owns an orange grove.

"Cat-o-lantern," 1993, by Carin Christerson, Santa Barbara, California, 42½" x 49½". Pieced and appliquéd by Carin Christerson; machine quilted by Christal Carter.

While still in high school, my oldest daughter, Carin, designed several Log Cabin quilts on graph paper. She recently decided it was time to complete one of those quilts. She selected her "Cat-o-lantern" design, and here you see the happy result! This is a wonderful, friendly child's quilt for autumn.

"Guardian Angel," 1993, by Christal Carter, Valley Center, California, 57" x 43". Pieced and appliquéd by Christal Carter; machine quilted by Irene Chang.

"Christmas Nativity," 1991, by Christal Carter, Valley Center, California, 19" x 19".

Soft colors and shiny lamé accents make this quilt a special keepsake for any little girl. Designed as a "celebration" quilt, this angel would be perfect for any little girl's birth, baptism, confirmation, or even graduation. It could also be a Christmas quilt with a few color changes.

This tiny nativity quilt is both quick and easy to make. Originally designed for a crafts periodical, this design has been requested by many students. Make one for each of the children on your holiday gift list.

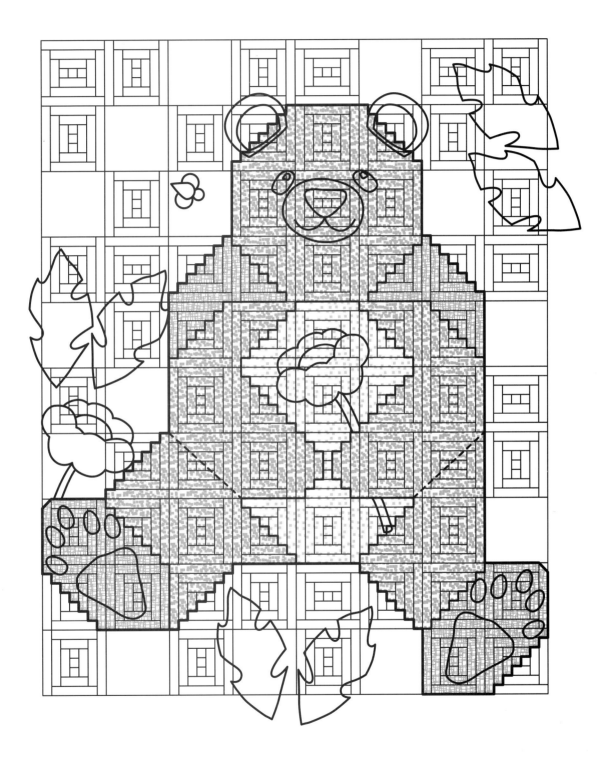

Photo: page 47 • Size: 36″ x 43″ • 80 Blocks • Finished Block Size: 3¹/₂″ x 3¹/₂″

Honey Bear

Traditional Blocks

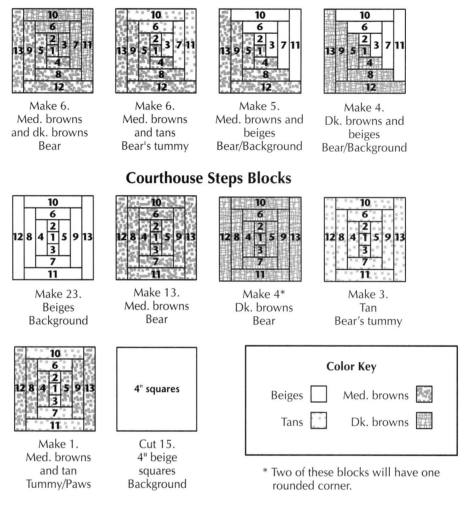

Make 6.
Med. browns
and dk. browns
Bear

Make 6.
Med. browns
and tans
Bear's tummy

Make 5.
Med. browns and
beiges
Bear/Background

Make 4.
Dk. browns and
beiges
Bear/Background

Courthouse Steps Blocks

Make 23.
Beiges
Background

Make 13.
Med. browns
Bear

Make 4*
Dk. browns
Bear

Make 3.
Tan
Bear's tummy

Make 1.
Med. browns
and tan
Tummy/Paws

4" squares

Cut 15.
4" beige
squares
Background

Color Key

| Beiges | ☐ | Med. browns | ▨ |
| Tans | ☐ | Dk. browns | ▨ |

* Two of these blocks will have one
rounded corner.

Materials: 44"- wide fabric

1¼ yds. total assorted beiges for back-
    ground, muzzle, and foot pads
¼ yd. tan for bear's tummy
¾ yd. total assorted medium browns for
    bear
⅓ yd. total assorted dark browns for bear
¼ yd. total of greens and browns for leaves
⅛ yd. burgundy for flowers
1⅓ yds. border print, with 4 repeats in the
    design, for border. (1⅓ yds. of any fabric
    may be used instead of a border print.)
2 yds. for binding and backing
Scrap of gold for flowers and bee
Scrap of black solid for eyes and nose

Notions: ½ yd. narrow green bias tape for flower
stems; black and white embroidery floss

Directions

1. Color in the quilt plan and blocks with
   colored pencils to help eliminate mistakes.
2. Make a sample block to test the accuracy of
   your seam allowance. The block should
   measure 4" square (it will be 3½" square
   when sewn into the quilt.)
3. Before cutting strips for blocks, be sure to
   reserve some of the beige for bear's muzzle
   and foot pads. Also, reserve some of each
   beige to cut a total of fifteen 4" squares.

4. Using either the speed-piecing method or templates, make the blocks shown on page 42. Notice that 2 of the dark brown Courthouse Steps blocks each have a "rounded" corner. (See page 11.) These form the tips of the bear's feet.

5. When all the blocks are completed, sew the blocks together in vertical rows as shown in the quilt plan on page 53. Sew the rows together, making sure to match the seams between each block.

6. Cut the border print into 4 lengthwise border strips. The length will be determined by the width of your border strip. If you are not using border print fabric, cut 4 strips, 4½" x 44".

7. Attach border strips to each side of the quilt and miter corners as shown on pages 84–85.

8. Using the templates (T-5 on the pullout patterns), complete the appliqué:
   muzzle, nose, and eyes to face
   ears to head
   foot pads to feet
   stems, flowers, leaves, and bee to background

9. Complete embroidery. See page 20 for embroidery stitches.
   mouth—black outline stitch, 2 rows
   "gleam" in eyes—white satin stitch
   lines between flower petals—black outline stitch
   lines to separate arms from body—black outline stitch
   bee's stripes and antennae—black outline stitch
   bee's eyes, nose, and antennae tips—black French knots

10. Mark the top for quilting. Mark veins on the leaves. Use designs of your choice for the background and border.

11. Layer the quilt top, batting, and backing. Pin or baste layers together. Quilt on marked lines and around bear, eyes, nose, muzzle, paws, arms, foot pads, flowers, leaves, and bee.

12. When quilting is complete, trim batting and backing to match quilt top. Bind edges with 2½"-wide strips of fabric, using the double-fold method on pages 87–88.

Toytime Teddy

Photo: page 48 • Size: 82″ x 92″ • 381 Blocks • Finished Block Size: 3¹/₂″ x 3¹/₂″

Traditional Blocks

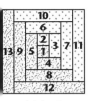

Make 2.
Med. browns,
lt. browns
Bear

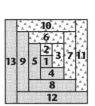

Make 4.
Reds, lt. reds
Balloon

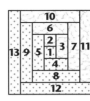

Make 5.
Lt. browns,
off-whites
Bear/Floor

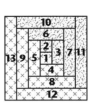

Make 4.
Lt. blues,
med. browns
Bear/Ribbon

Make 3.
Dk. blues,
off-white print
Balloon/Wall

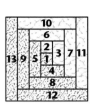

Make 3.
Med. browns,
off-whites
Bear/Floor

Make 3.
Lt. browns,
dk. browns
Bear paw

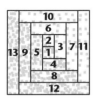

Make 3.
Golds,
yellows
Balloon

Make 4.
Med. browns,
dk. browns
Bear/Wheels

Make 9.
Lt. browns,
med. browns
Bear

Make 2.
Dk. blues,
lt. blues
Balloon

Make 2.
Dk. greens,
lt. greens
Balloon

Make 3.
Dk. browns,
off-whites
Bear/Floor

Make 2.
Med. browns,
dk. reds
Bear/Floor

Make 2.
Yellows,
off-white print
Balloon/Wall

Make 2.
White,
lt. yellows
Balloon

Make 2.
White,
lt. blues
Balloon

Make 2.
White, lt. reds
Balloon

Make 2.
Dk. reds,
dk. browns
Paw/Foot

Make 2.
Med. browns,
off-white print
Bear/Wall

Make 2.
Lt. blues,
dk. blues
Bow

Make 2.
Lt. blues,
off-white print
and beige
Balloon/Wall

Make 2.
Dk. reds, off-white
print and beige
Balloon/Wall

Make 1.
Golds, lt. greens
Balloon

Make 1.
White, lt. greens
Balloon

Make 1.
Lt. browns,
dk. reds
Paw

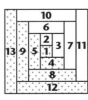

Make 1.
Lt. browns,
off-white print
Bear/Wall

Make 5.
Lt. blues,
lt. browns
Bear/Ribbon

Make 2.
Lt. blues,
off-white
Block/Ribbon

Make 1.
Dk. browns,
lt. browns
Bear foot

Toytime Teddy

Traditional Blocks (continued)

Make 1.
Lt. reds,
off-white print
Balloon

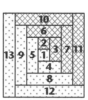

Make 1.
Lt. blues,
off-white print
Ribbon

Make 1.
Lt. browns,
dk. blues
Bear/Ribbon

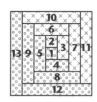

Make 1.
Lt. greens,
off-whites
Block

Make 1.
Lt. greens,
lt. blues
Block

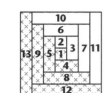

Make 1.
Lt. reds,
lt. blues
Balloon

Make 1.
Golds, lt. reds
Balloon

Make 1.
Lt. reds,
dk. greens
Balloons

Make 1.
Dk. greens,
off-white print
Balloon

Make 1.
Lt. blues,
dk. blues
Ribbon

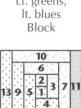

Make 1.
Lt. browns,
off-whites and
dk. reds
Bear/Floor

Make 1.
Med. browns,
off-white print
and beige
Bear/Wall

Make 1.
Dk. brown,
lt. browns,
off-whites
Foot

Make 1.
Lt. browns,
dk. reds and
off-white print
Ear

Courthouse Steps Blocks

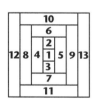

Make 37.
Off-white
print
Wallpaper

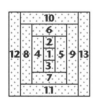

Make 37.
Lt. browns
Bear

Make 22.
Off-white
print, beige
Wallpaper

Make 21.
Dk. reds
Balloon/Floor

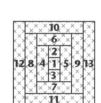

Make 14.
Lt. blues
Balloons/
Ribbon/Block

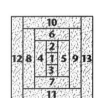

Make 14.
Med. browns
Bear

Make 13.
Lt. reds
Balloon

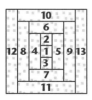

Make 13.
Yellows
Balloon

Make 11.
Off-whites
Floor

Make 10.
Golds
Balloon/Car

Make 6.
Dk. browns
Bear

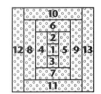

Make 5.
Lt. greens
Balloon/Block

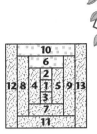

Courthouse Steps Blocks (continued)

Make 4.
Dk. greens
Block

Make 3.
Dk. blues
Balloons

Make 3.
Off-whites,
dk. reds
Floor

Make 2.
Golds, black
Car

Make 1.
Lt. browns,
off-white print
Ear

Make 1.
Med. browns,
yellows
Ear

  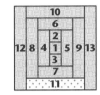

Make 1.
Tan,
lt. browns
Ear

Make 1.
Tan, med.
browns
Ear

Make 1.
Dk. reds,
lt. browns
Ear

Make 1.
Golds, med.
browns
Ear

Make 1.
Lt. blues, dk.
blues
Ribbon

Make 1.
Lt. browns,
dk. blues
Ribbon

Make 1.
Med. browns,
golds
Car window

Unusual Blocks

    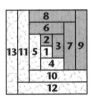

Make 2.
Med. browns,
off-white print
and beige
Bear/Wall

Make 2.
Lt. browns,
black
Eyes

Make 2.
Dk. browns,
black
Nose

Make 4.
Black, rust and
med. browns
Tires

Make 2.
Black, dk. reds
Tires

Make 2.
Black, off-whites
Tires

   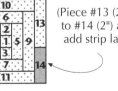

Make 1.
Lt. browns,
dk. browns
Chin

Make 1.
Lt. browns,
dk. browns
Chin

Make 1.
Lt. blues,
off-white print
and beige
Balloon/Wall

Make 1.
Dk. reds, dk.
blues and
lt. blues
Balloon

Make 1.
Lt. browns,
black
Top of car

(Piece #13 (2½")
to #14 (2") and
add strip last.)

Unusual Blocks (continued)

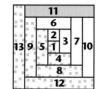

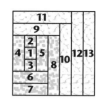

Make 1.
Lt. greens,
off-white print
and beige
Balloon/Wall

Make 1.
Yellows,
off-white print
and beige
Balloon/Wall

Make 1.
Golds,
off-white print
and beige
Balloon/Wall

Make 1.
Lt. browns,
off-white print
and beige
Bear/Wall

Make 1.
Golds,
off-whites
Rear of car

Make 1.
Golds, dk.
reds
Rear of car

Alphabet and Number Blocks

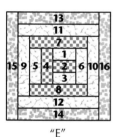
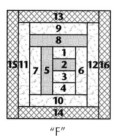
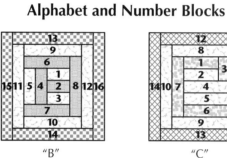
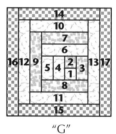
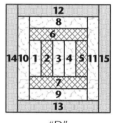
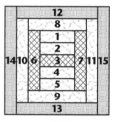

"A"
Piece #1: 1" x 2"

"B"
Piece #1: 1" x 1½"

"C"
Piece #1: 1" x 2"

"D"
Piece #1: 1" x 2"

"E"
Piece #1: 1" x 1½"

"F"
Piece #1: 1" x 1½"

"G"
Piece #1: 1" x 1"

"H"
Piece #1: 1" x 2"

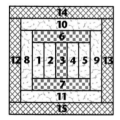
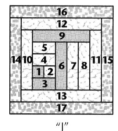
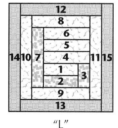
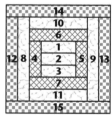

"I"
Piece #1: 1" x 2"

"J"
Piece #1: 1" x 1"

"L"
Piece #1: 1" x 2"

"O"
Piece #1: 1" x 2"

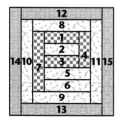
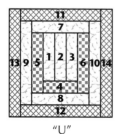
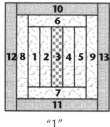

"P"
Piece #1: 1" x 2"

"U"
Piece #1: 1" x 2½"

"1"
Piece #1: 1" x 3"

"6"
Piece #1: 1" x 2"

Alphabet and Number Blocks (continued)

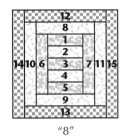

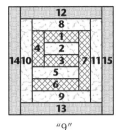

"8"
Piece #1: 1" x 2"

"9"
Piece #1: 1" x 2"

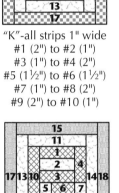

"K"-all strips 1" wide
#1 (2") to #2 (1")
#3 (1") to #4 (2")
#5 (1½") to #6 (1½")
#7 (1") to #8 (2")
#9 (2") to #10 (1")

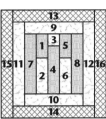

"M"-all strips 1" wide
#1 (1½") to #2 (2")
#3 (1") to #4 (2½")
#5 (1½") to #6 (2")
Sew these together,
then add #7, and so on.

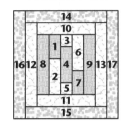

"N"-all strips 1" wide
#1 (1½") to #2 (2")
#3 (1") to #4 (2") to #5 (1")
#6 (2") to #7 (1½")
Sew these together, then
add #8, and so on.

"Q"-all strips 1" wide
#1 (1") to #2 (1") to #3 (1")
#11 (2") to #12 (1") to #13 (1")
Sew unit 1/2/3 to piece #4,
and so on.

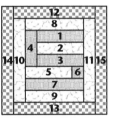

"R"-all strips 1" wide
#1,#2, #3 (2") #5 (1") to
#6 (1½") to #7 (1")
#8 (1½") to #9 (1½")
Sew pieces 1–4 in order, add
unit 5/6/7, then unit 8/9,
and so on.

"S"-all strips 1" wide
#1, #2, #3 (2½")
#5 (2½") to #6 (1")
Sew pieces 1–4 in
order, add unit 5/6
and continue in order.

"T"-all strips 1" wide
#1, #2, #3 (2½")
#4 (1") to #5 (2")
#6 (1") to #7 (2")
Sew pieces 1–3, then
add unit 4/5 and unit
6/7; continue piecing
in order.

"V"-all strips 1" wide
#1 (2") to #2 (1½")
#3 (1½") to #4 (1½") to #5 (1")
#6 (2") to #7 (1½")
#8 (1½") to #9 (1½") to #10 (1")
#11 (2") to #12 (1½")
Piece units together;
continue piecing in order.

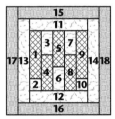

"W"-all strips 1" wide
#1 (2½") to #2 (1")
#3 (1½") to #4 (2")
#5 (2") to #6 (1½")
#7 (1½") to #8 (2")
#9 (2½") to #10 (1")
Sew units together and
continue piecing in order.

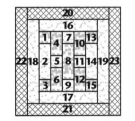

"X"-all strips 1" wide
#1 (1") to #2 (2") to #3 (1")
#4 (1½") to #5 (1") to #6 (1½")
#7 (1") to #8 (2") to #9 (1")
#10 (1½") to #11 (1") to #12 (1½")
#13 (1") to #14 (2") to #15 (1")
Sew units together and continue
piecing in order.

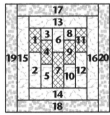

"Y"-all strips 1" wide
#1 (1½") to #2 (2")
#3 (1") to #4 (1½") to #5 (1½")
#6 (1½") to #7 (2")
#8 (1") to #9 (1½") to #10 (1½")
#11 (1½") to #12 (2")
#13 (1") to #14 (2") to #15 (1")
Sew units together and continue
piecing in order.

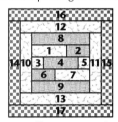

"Z"-all strips 1" wide
#1 (2") to #2 (1½")
#3 (1") to #4 (2") to #5 (1")
#6 (1½") to #7 (2")
Sew units together and
continue piecing in order.

Toytime Teddy

Alphabet and Number Blocks (continued)

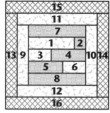

"2"-all strips 1" wide
#1 (2½") to #2 (1")
#3 (1½") to #4 (2")
#5 (2") to #6 (1½")
Sew units together and
continue piecing in order.

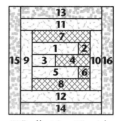

"3"-all strips 1" wide
#1 (2½") to #2 (1")
#3 (1½") to #4 (2")
#5 (2½") to #6 (1")
Sew units together and
continue piecing in order.

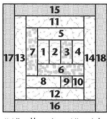

"4"-all strips 1" wide
#1, #2, #3, #4 (1½")
#8 (2") to #9 (1") to #10 (1")
Sew pieces 1–7, then add
unit 8/9/10 and continue
piecing in order.

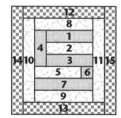

"5"-all strips 1" wide
#1, #2, #3 (2½")
#5 (2½") to #6 (1")
Sew pieces 1–4, then add
unit 5/6 and continue
piecing in order.

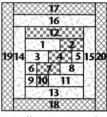

"7"-all strips 1" wide
#1 (2") to #2 (1½")
#3 (1½") to #4 (1½") to #5 (1")
#6 (1") to #7 (1½") to #8 (1½")
#9 (1") to #10 (1") to #11 (2")
Sew units together and continue
piecing in order.

Color Key

White	Dk. reds	Dk. browns	Off-white print
Black	Lt. greens	Lt. yellows	
Lt. blues	Dk. greens	Golds	Tan
Dk. blues	Lt. browns	Beige	Rust
Lt. reds	Med. browns	Off-whites	

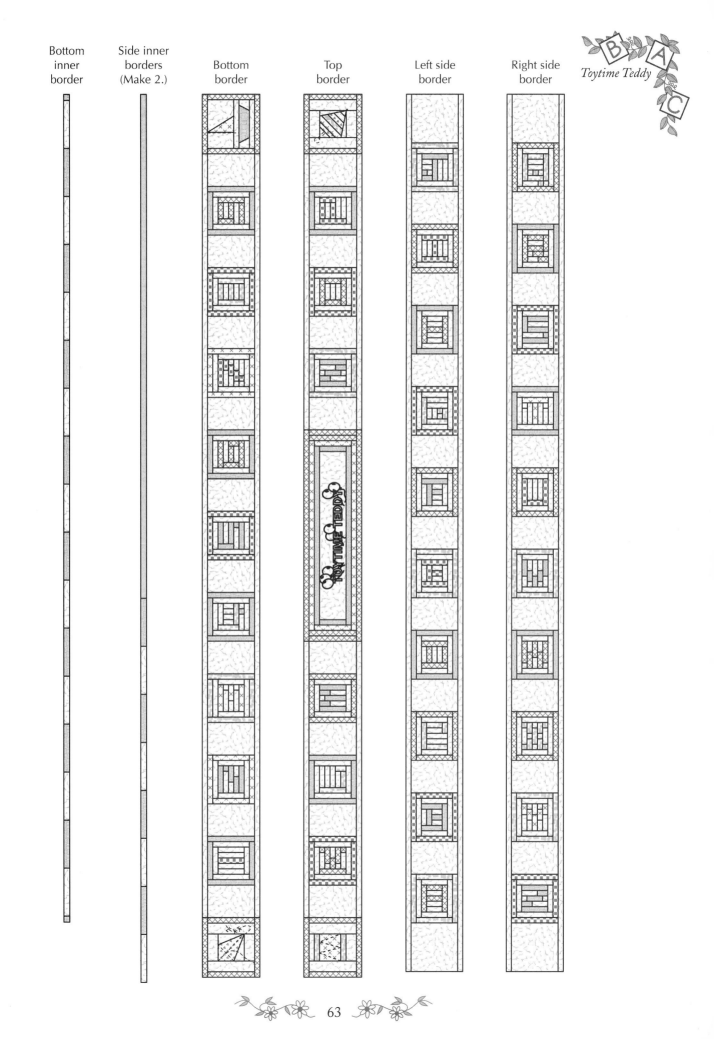

Bottom inner border

Side inner borders (Make 2.)

Bottom border

Top border

Left side border

Right side border

Toytime Teddy

Materials: 44"- wide fabric

2 yds. off-white print for wallpaper

1⅞ yds. total assorted light browns for bear

1 yd. total assorted medium browns for shadows on bear

½ yd. total assorted dark browns for paws and muzzle

2¾ yds. total off-whites for floor and alphabet

⅞ yd. total assorted light blues for balloons, ribbon, and block

½ yd. total assorted dark blues for balloons, ribbon, and alphabet

½ yd. total assorted yellows for balloons

¾ yd. total assorted golds for balloons, car, and alphabet

⅝ yd. total assorted light reds for balloons

1¼ yds. total assorted dark reds for balloons, floor, and alphabet

⅓ yd. total assorted light greens for balloon and block

⅜ yd. total assorted dark greens for balloon, block, and alphabet

⅓ yd. beige for stripes in wallpaper

¼ yd. black for tires, car roof, eyes, and nose

⅛ yd. white for "shine" on balloons

1⅝ yds. dark brown for border

6¼ yds. for backing and binding

Scrap of tan for inner ears and steering wheel

Scrap of rust for wheel wells

Notions: white, red, yellow, blue, green, and black embroidery floss; black pearl cotton

Directions

Block Assembly

1. Color in the quilt plan and blocks with colored pencils to help eliminate mistakes.
2. Make a sample block to test the accuracy of your seam allowance. The block should measure 4" square (it will be 3½" square when sewn into the quilt). The alphabet blocks should measure 5" square (4½" square when sewn into the borders). The 4 corner blocks (T-7, T-8, T-9, and T-10 on the pullout patterns) in the borders should measure 6" square (5½" when sewn into the quilt). Reserve fabric for appliquéd block letters and corner "toy" blocks before cutting fabric into strips.
3. Using either the speed-piecing method or templates, make the blocks shown on pages 57–62. Set aside 2 of the medium brown/dark brown Traditional blocks for appliquéd wheels. Set aside the 4 Toy blocks, as well as the Alphabet and Number blocks.
4. Sew the remaining 4" blocks together in vertical rows as shown in the quilt plan on page 56. Sew the rows together, making sure to match the seams between each block.

Alphabet and Number Blocks

To piece the Alphabet and Number blocks, cut 1"-wide strips in the color and length indicated for each block in the block diagrams on pages 60–62. For example, to make the letter "A," cut the first strip 2" long. The diagram shows that strip #1 is blue. Sew a 1" x 2" blue strip to an off-white strip. Trim the off-white strip to match piece #1. Keep adding strips in the order and color indicated. Trim to match the previous strip. Finished blocks will be 5" square (4½" square when sewn into the quilt.)

Note: Some blocks, such as the K block, require you to piece a strip lengthwise before adding it to the unit. Diagrams for these specially pieced blocks are shown on pages 60–62.

Borders and Finishing

1. For the pieced side and bottom inner border strips, cut:

   16 dark red strips, 1" x 4", for floor
   2 dark red squares, 1" x 1", for floor
   17 off-white strips, 1" x 4", for floor
   2 beige strips, 1" x 42½", for wallpaper stripe

2. Piece the side and bottom strips as shown on page 63. Sew the side strips to the quilt, making sure to match seams in the checkered floor area. Sew the bottom strip to the quilt, matching seams.

3. For the dark brown middle border, cut:

   4 strips, 5½" x 71" (piece strips to obtain length)
   2 strips, 1" x 83"
   2 strips, 1" x 93" (reserve for final border)

4. Sew the 5½"-wide dark brown strips to the sides, then to the top and bottom of the quilt.

5. Before adding the alphabet border, complete all the embroidery and appliqué on the quilt. Using the templates (T-6 on the pullout patterns), complete the appliqué:

   letters to block
   circles to wheels (cut from 2 extra Traditional blocks)
   headlight to car front
   steering wheel inside window
   ball pull near block
   bottoms to balloons
   center of bow to ribbon

6. Complete the embroidery. See page 20 for embroidery stitches.

   steering wheel and post—black outline stitch
   wheel centers—black outline stitch
   car door handle—black satin stitch
   bear's smile—black outline stitch using pearl cotton
   "gleam" in bear's eyes—white satin stitch

   balloon strings—black outline stitch using pearl cotton
   toy car string—black outline stitch using pearl cotton
   mast in sailboat block—black outline stitch
   lines on drum in drum block—black outline stitch
   handle and tip in top block—black satin stitch
   string in kite block—black outline stitch

   "Toytime Teddy" block. Cut a 7" x 20" strip from off-white. Trace the "Toytime Teddy" embroidery pattern (T-6 on the pullout patterns) onto the off-white strip. Use a black outline stitch for the balloon strings. Use a red outline stitch for letters.

7. For the pieced alphabet border, cut the following from off-white (piece strips to obtain length):

   4 strips, 1" x 81", for side borders
   2 strips, 1" x 71", for bottom border
   4 strips, 1" x 26", for top border
   36 rectangles, 3½" x 5", for spacers between letters and numbers
   4 pieces, 4¾" x 5", for the ends of side borders

   Trim the embroidered "Toytime Teddy" block to 16" x 3".

8. Follow the diagram on page 63 to piece the alphabet and number border. Use 9 of the 3½" x 5" off-white rectangles, 2 of the 4¾" x 5" off-white pieces, 2 of the 1" x 81" off-white strips, and A–J of the Alphabet blocks. Sew border to the left side of the quilt.

9. Using 9 of the 3½" x 5" off-white rectangles and Alphabet blocks Q–Z, piece the second side border as shown. Sew the border to the right side of the quilt.

10. Using 10 of the 3½" x 5" off-white rectangles, the two 1" x 71" off-white strips, the Number blocks, and the Kite and Boat corner blocks, piece the bottom border as shown. Sew the border to the bottom of the quilt.

11. Cut the following strips to border the embroidered "Toytime Teddy" block:

    From red, cut:
        2 strips, 1" x 3"
        2 strips, 1" x 17"
    From light blue, cut:
        2 strips, 1" x 4"
        2 strips, 1" x 18"
    From dark blue, cut:
        4 strips, 1" x 5"
        2 strips, 1" x 20"

    Following the piecing sequence in the top-border diagram on page 63, sew these strips to the embroidered block.

12. Using 8 of the 3½" x 5" off-white strips, the four 1" x 26" off-white strips, the remaining Alphabet blocks, the "Toytime Teddy" block, and the Top and Drum blocks, piece the upper border. Refer to the border plans on page 63. Sew to the top of the quilt.

13. Using the remaining 1"-wide dark brown strips, sew the 92"-long strips to the quilt sides, and the 82"-long strips to the top and bottom.

14. Mark the top for quilting. Mark Xs in the checkered Floor blocks, curved Xs between the Number and Alphabet blocks, and evenly spaced parallel lines in dark brown border.

15. Layer the quilt top, batting, and backing. Pin or baste layers together. Quilt on marked lines, around every object, and around all numbers and letters. Quilt within teddy as desired.

16. When quilting is complete, trim batting and backing to match the quilt top. Bind the edges with 2½"-wide strips of fabric, using the double-fold method on pages 87–88.

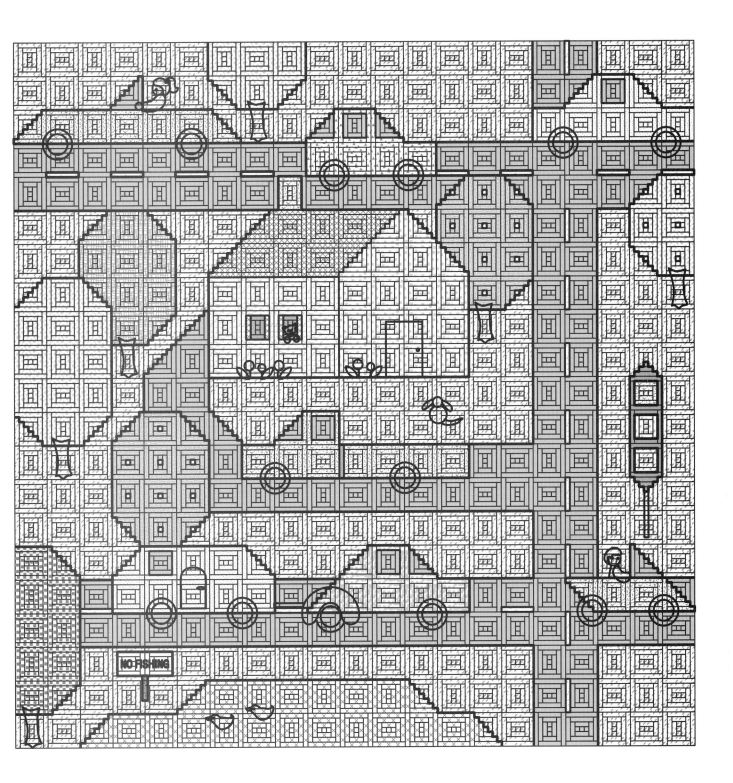

Photo: page 49 • Size: 87¹/₂″ x 87¹/₂″ • 441 Blocks • Finished Block Size: 3¹/₂″ x 3¹/₂″

Stop and Go

Traditional Blocks

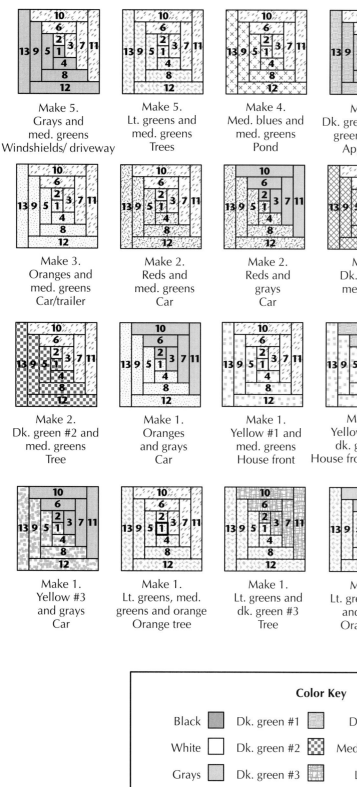
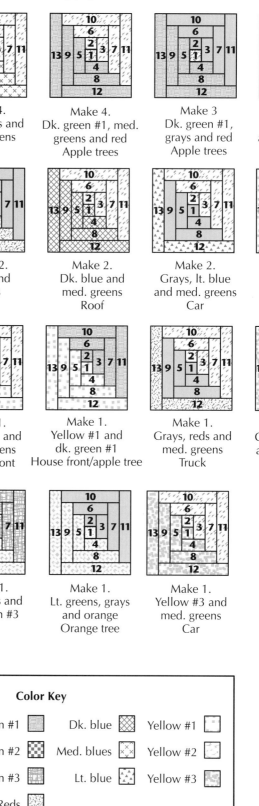

Make 5.
Grays and
med. greens
Windshields/ driveway

Make 5.
Lt. greens and
med. greens
Trees

Make 4.
Med. blues and
med. greens
Pond

Make 4.
Dk. green #1, med.
greens and red
Apple trees

Make 3.
Dk. green #1,
grays and red
Apple trees

Make 3.
Dk. green #3
and med. greens
Tree

Make 3.
Oranges and
med. greens
Car/trailer

Make 2.
Reds and
med. greens
Car

Make 2.
Reds and
grays
Car

Make 2.
Dk. blue and
med. greens
Roof

Make 2.
Grays, lt. blue
and med. greens
Car

Make 2.
Yellow #1 and
dk. blue
Roof

Make 2.
Dk. green #2 and
med. greens
Tree

Make 1.
Oranges
and grays
Car

Make 1.
Yellow #1 and
med. greens
House front

Make 1.
Yellow #1 and
dk. green #1
House front/apple tree

Make 1.
Grays, reds and
med. greens
Truck

Make 1.
Grays, yellow #3
and med. greens
Car

Make 1.
Yellow #3
and grays
Car

Make 1.
Lt. greens, med.
greens and orange
Orange tree

Make 1.
Lt. greens and
dk. green #3
Tree

Make 1.
Lt. greens, grays
and orange
Orange tree

Make 1.
Yellow #3 and
med. greens
Car

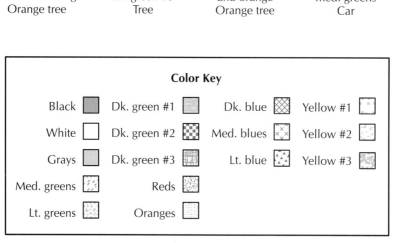

Color Key

Black		Dk. green #1		Dk. blue	Yellow #1
White		Dk. green #2		Med. blues	Yellow #2
Grays		Dk. green #3		Lt. blue	Yellow #3
Med. greens		Reds			
Lt. greens		Oranges			

68

Courthouse Steps Blocks

 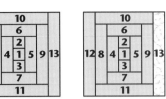 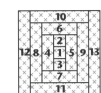

Make 144.
Med. greens
Grass

Make 83.
Grays
Road

Make 20.
Grays and
yellow #2
Road

Make 17.
Med. blues
Pond

Make 15.
Dk. green #1
and red
Apple trees

Make 15.
Lt. greens
Trees

Make 14.
Yellow #1
House front

Make 13.
Reds
Cars/Trucks

Make 12.
Oranges
Trailer/Car

Make 10.
Yellow #2
House side

Make 8.
Dk. green #2
Tree

Make 7.
Dk. green #3
Tree

Make 6.
Dk. blue
Roof

Make 4.
Yellow #3
Car

Make 4.
Lt. blue
Car

Make 4.
Lt. greens and
oranges
Orange tree

Make 2.
Grays and oranges
Car/trailer
windows

Make 2.
Black, dk. blue
and yellow #2
House windows

 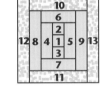

Make 2.
White and
med. greens
Sign

Make 2.
Med. greens
and black
Stoplight

Make 1.
Grays and
yellow #3
Car window

Make 1.
Grays and
lt. blue
Car window

Make 1.
Reds and black
Stoplight

Make 1.
Yellow #2 and
black
Stoplight

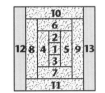

Make 1.
Med. greens
and black
Stoplight

Make 1.
Reds and gray
Chimney

Make 1.
Reds and grays
Truck window

Make 1.
Reds and
black
Truck

Stop and Go

Materials: 44"- wide fabric

4³/₄ yds. total assorted medium greens for grass and stoplight

3½ yds. total assorted grays for roads and windshields

⅝ yd. light green for 3 trees

⅝ yd. dark green #1 for apple trees

⅓ yd. dark green #2 for tree beside pond

⅓ yd. dark green #3 for tree beside house

⅝ yd. total assorted reds for vehicles, chimney, door, stoplight, and apple trees

½ yd. total assorted oranges for trailer, car, and orange trees

½ yd. yellow #1 for house front

½ yd. yellow #2 for house side, road, stoplight and fender

¼ yd. yellow #3 for car

¼ yd. dark blue for roof and girl's blouse

½ yd. total assorted medium blues for pond

⅛ yd. light blue for car, trailer door, and boy's shirt

¼ yd. black for tires and house windows

⅛ yd. white print for hubcaps

2 yds. coordinating print for border (more fabric may be required if you select a directional print)

5½ yds. for backing and binding

Scraps of the following fabrics:
Light gray for sign
Brown for tree trunks
Skin-tone colors for people

Notions: Black, orange, and red embroidery floss

Directions

1. Color in the quilt plan and blocks with colored pencils to help eliminate mistakes.
2. Make a sample block to test the accuracy of your seam allowance. The block should measure 4" square (it will be 3½" square when sewn into the quilt).
3. Before making the blocks, reserve enough of the red for the house door and yellow #2 for car fender.

4. Using either the speed-piecing method or templates, make the blocks shown on pages 68–69.
5. When all the blocks are completed, sew the blocks together in horizontal rows as shown in the quilt plan on page 67. Sew the rows together, making sure to match the seams between each block.
6. For borders, cut 4 strips from the printed border fabric, each measuring 7¼" x 90" (piece strips to obtain length). If you use a directional print, such as the one shown on page 67, you might need to cut two borders from the lengthwise grain of the fabric and two from the crosswise grain of the fabric.
7. Attach border strips to each side of the quilt and miter corners as shown on pages 84–85.
8. Using the templates (T-11 on the pullout patterns), complete the appliqué:
    wheels and hubcaps to vehicles
    fender to yellow car
    trunks to trees
    door to house
    kitten and paws to window
    flowers and leaves to house
    dog to yard
    girl to upper red sports car
    boy to lower red sports car
    ducks to pond
    pole to stoplight
    signpost to sign
    trailer hitch between trailer and car
    door to trailer
9. Complete the embroidery. See page 20 for embroidery stitches.
    eyes of people—black satin stitch
    cat's face—black outline stitch with black satin stitch nose
    flower stems—black outline stitch
    ducks' beaks—orange satin stitch
    ducks' eyes—black satin stitch
    words "NO FISHING" on sign—black outline stitch
    car door handles—black outline stitch
    door knob—black satin stitch

10. Mark the top for quilting. Mark vertical zigzags in all grass areas, ripples in the pond, and scallops in the trees. Draw evenly spaced vertical lines in the yellow areas of the house. Draw evenly spaced horizontal lines in the house's blue roof. Mark the border as desired (consider drawing little cars and trucks).

11. Layer the quilt top, batting, and backing. Pin or baste layers together. Quilt on all marked lines and around each vehicle, tree, person, animal, window, and door. Quilt in-the-ditch along each road and driveway and around each yellow road line. Quilt within vehicles to show fenders and other details.

12. When quilting is complete, trim batting and backing to match quilt top. Bind edges with 2½"-wide strips of fabric, using the double-fold method on pages 87–88.

The Old Oak Tree

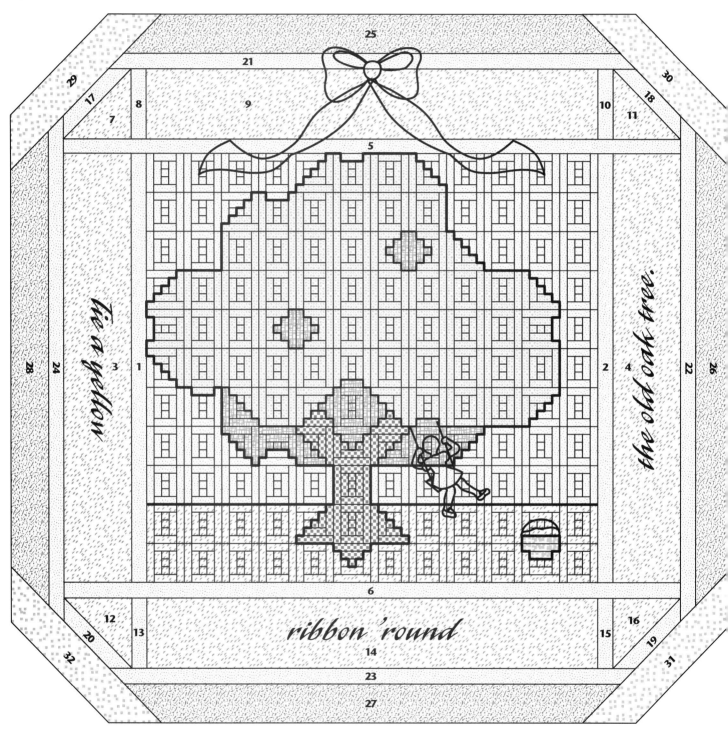

Photo: page 50 • Size: 44¹/₂″ x 47″ • 132 Blocks • Finished Block Size: 2¹/₂″ x 2¹/₂″

Traditional Blocks

Make 8. Med. greens and lt. blues Tree/Sky	Make 2. Browns and grass green Tree trunk/Grass	Make 2. Dk. greens and lt. blues Tree/Sky	Make 2. Browns and dk. greens Tree trunk	Make 1. Med. greens, browns and dk. greens Tree trunk	Make 1. Med. greens, browns and dk. greens Tree trunk	Make 1. Dk. greens and Med. greens Tree

Courthouse Steps Blocks

Make 40. Lt. blues Sky	Make 37. Med. greens Tree	Make 18. Grass green Grass	Make 4. Med. greens and dk. greens Tree	Make 4. Med greens and lt. blues Tree/Sky	Make 2. Dk. greens Tree	Make 2. Med. greens and dk. greens Tree

    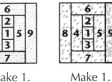

Make 2. Browns Trunk	Make 1. Grass green and browns Trunk /Grass	Make 1. Browns and dk. greens Trunk	Make 1. Dk. greens and lt. blues Tree/Sky	Make 1. Lt. blues and med. greens Tree/Sky	Make 1. Grass green and brown plaid Basket	Make 1. Grass green and brown plaid Basket

Color Key

Grass green	▦	Dk. greens	▦	Lt. blues	☐
Med. greens	☐	Yellow	▦	Yellow print	☐
Browns	▦	Brown plaid	▦		

Materials: 44"- wide fabric

¾ yd. total assorted medium greens for tree
¾ yd. total assorted light blues for sky
⅓ yd. grass green (different from tree fabrics)
⅛ yd. total assorted dark greens for shadows in tree
⅛ yd. total assorted browns for tree trunk
¼ yd. yellow print for bow, dress, and border corners
¾ yd. green print for border
½ yd. medium blue for border
⅜ yd. yellow for border and ribbon
3¼ yds. for backing
Scraps of skin-tone fabric for girl and brown plaid for basket, red print for cloth on basket, dark gold for inner bow

Notions: black, brown, red, pink, yellow, gold, dark green, and beige embroidery floss; ½ yd. of ⅓"-wide yellow ribbon for bow on tree trunk

The Old Oak Tree

Directions

1. Color in the quilt plan and blocks with colored pencils to help eliminate mistakes.
2. Make a sample block to test the accuracy of your seam allowance. The block should measure 3" square (it will be 2½" square when sewn into the quilt).
3. Using either the speed-piecing method or templates, make blocks shown on page 73.
4. When all of the blocks are completed, sew the blocks together in horizontal rows as shown in the quilt plan on page 72. Sew the rows together, making sure to match the seams between each block.
5. Cut the following strips for the borders. Strips with a diagonal end are cut slightly longer than needed; you will trim these after adding them to the quilt.

    From green for border, cut:
       2 strips, 5" x 28"
       2 strips, 5" x 30½"
       2 squares, 5⅜"x 5⅜". Cut each square once diagonally to make a total of 4 triangles.
    From medium blue, cut:
       2 strips, 1½" x 28"
       2 strips, 1½" x 41½"
       4 strips, 1½" x 5"
       4 strips, 1½" x 7"
       2 strips, 1½" x 31"
       2 strips, 1½" x 34"
    From the yellow, cut:
       2 strips, 3" x 31"
       2 strips, 3" x 34"
    From the yellow print, cut:
       4 strips, 3" x 12"

6. Sew the borders to the quilt, following the numbered sequence shown in the quilt plan on page 72. Add borders 1–6. Piece sections 7–11 and add to top of quilt. Piece sections 12–16 and add to bottom of quilt. Add corners 17–20 and trim excess fabric even with sides of quilt top. Add strips 21–28 and trim excess fabric even with the diagonal blue strips. Add the last 4 corners, 29–32, and trim excess fabric even with sides.

7. Using the templates (T-12 on the pullout patterns), complete the appliqué:
    swing seat to background
    girl's body, then dress, to swing seat
    red print to top of basket
    ribbons, then bow, to top center of quilt (Add yellow ribbon to tree trunk when quilting is complete.)
8. Complete the embroidery. See page 20 for embroidery stitches.
    girl's shoes—black satin stitch
    girl's hair—rows of alternating yellow and gold outline stitch
    hair bows and bow on dress—red detached chain stitches
    nose, eyebrows, and eyelashes—black outline stitch
    cheeks—pink satin stitch
    lips—red satin stitch
    swing rope—2 or 3 rows of beige outline stitch
    basket handle—2 or 3 rows of brown outline stitch
    buttons—red French knots
    tulips—red and green satin stitch
    words in border ("Tie a yellow ribbon 'round the old oak tree.")—green outline stitch
9. Mark the top for quilting. Draw wavy "wind" lines in sky, irregular scallops in the tree, and vertical zigzags in the grass. Mark evenly spaced cross-hatch grid lines in the border.
10. Layer quilt top, batting, and backing. Pin or baste layers together. Quilt on marked lines and around tree, girl, and basket. Tie a bow with yellow ribbon and tack to tree trunk.
11. When quilting is complete, trim batting and backing ½" smaller than quilt top. Fold front edge of outer border to back, leaving a 2"-wide border on the quilt front. Trim batting and backing as necessary. Fold under the raw edges of the border and slipstitch to quilt back.

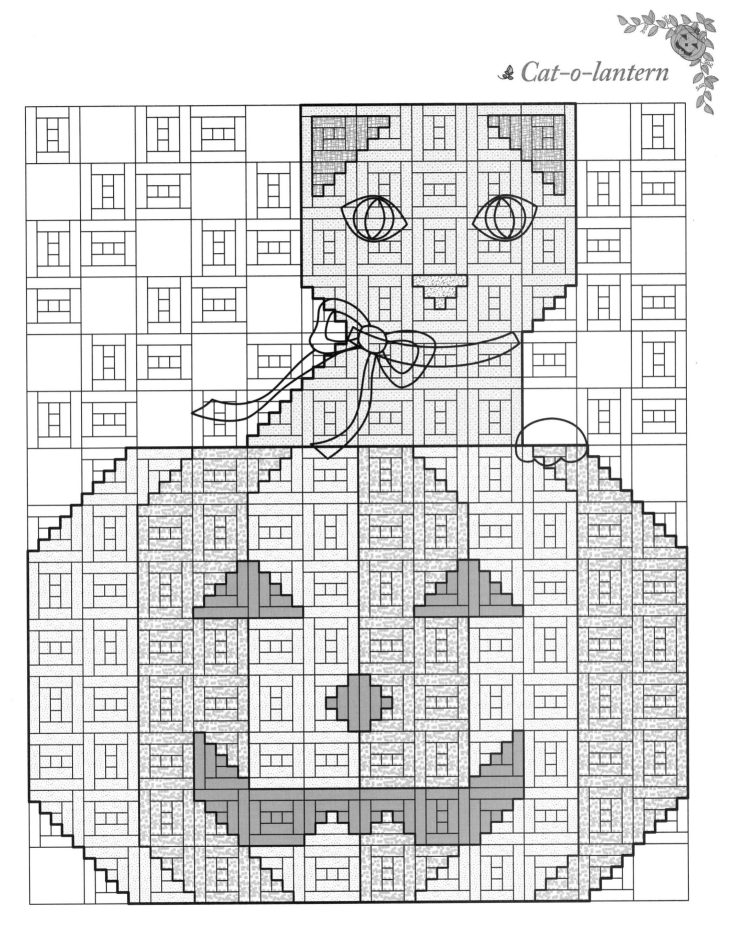

Photo: page 51 • Size: 42¹/₂″ x 49¹/₂″ • 168 Blocks • Finished Block Size: 2¹/₂″ x 2¹/₂″

Traditional Blocks

Make 8.
Med. oranges
and dk. orange
Pumpkin

Make 4.
Black solid and
dk. orange
Pumpkin

Make 4.
Black solid and
med. oranges
Pumpkin

Make 4.
Med. oranges
and creams
Pumpkin/
Background

Make 4.
Dk. orange
and creams
Pumpkin/
Background

Make 4.
Black prints
and creams
Cat/Background

Make 2.
Lt. browns
and black
prints
Ear tips

Make 2.
Black prints
and lt. brown
Ears

Courthouse Steps Blocks

Make 31.
Dk. orange
Pumpkin

Make 31.
Med. oranges
Pumpkin

Make 29.
Creams
Background

Make 18.
Black prints
Cat

Make 2.
Black solid
Pumpkin's
mouth

Make 1.
Black prints
and tan
Cat's nose

Make 1.
Black solid and
dk. orange
Pumpkin's
tooth

   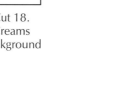

Make 1.
Black solid and
med. oranges
Pumpkin's tooth

Make 1.
Black solid and
dk. orange
Pumpkin nose

Make 1.
Black solid and
med. oranges
Pumpkin nose

Cut 18.
Creams
Background

Unusual Blocks

Make 2.
Black prints
and lt. brown
Cat's ears

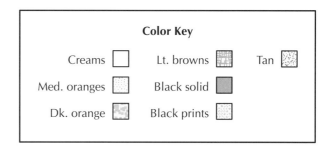

Materials: 44"- wide fabric

⅞ yd. total assorted creams for background

⅔ yd. total assorted medium oranges for pumpkin

⅔ yd. dark orange for pumpkin

½ yd. total assorted black prints for cat

⅓ yd. black solid for pumpkin's face and border

⅛ yd. black plaid or other dark print for floor

⅞ yd. coordinating print for border

1⅞ yds. for backing and binding

Scraps of the following fabrics:

    Light brown for cat's ears

    Tan for cat's nose

    Yellow-green for cat's eyes

    Avocado green for cat's eyes

    Light oranges for cat's bow

Notions: white embroidery floss

Directions

1. Color in the quilt plan and blocks with colored pencils to help eliminate mistakes.

2. Make a sample block to test the accuracy of your seam allowance. The block should measure 3" square (it will be 2½" square when sewn into the quilt.)

3. Using either the speed-piecing method or templates, make blocks shown on page 76.

4. When all of the blocks are completed, sew the blocks together in vertical rows as shown in the quilt plan on page 75. Sew the rows together, making sure to match the seams between each block.

5. Sew a 1" x 35½" cream strip to each side of the quilt. Then sew a 1" x 31½" cream strip to the top of the quilt. Sew a 3" x 31½" black plaid strip to the bottom of the quilt.

6. Sew one 1" x 38½" solid black strip to each side of the quilt. Sew one 1" x 33" solid black strip to the top and bottom of the quilt.

7. From the border print, cut:
   2 strips, 5½" x 52" (piece strips to get length)
   2 strips, 5½" x 45"

8. Attach border strips to each side of the quilt and miter corners as shown on pages 84–85.

9. Using the templates (T-13 on the pullout patterns), complete the appliqué:
   neckband, sashes, and bow to cat's neck
   eyes to cat's face
   cat's paw to pumpkin

10. Complete the embroidery. (See embroidery stitches on page 20.) Use a white satin stitch for the "gleam" in the cat's eyes.

11. Mark the top for quilting. Mark vertical curves where the pumpkin oranges change color. Draw evenly spaced cross-hatch grid lines in the background.

12. Layer the quilt top, batting and backing. Pin or baste layers together. Quilt on marked lines, around cat and pumpkin, and around features of cat and pumpkin.

13. When quilting is complete, trim batting and backing to match quilt top. Bind edges with 2½"-wide strips of fabric, using the double-fold method on pages 87–88.

Photo: page 52 • Size: 57" x 43" • 165 Blocks • Finished Block Size: 3½" x 3½"

Traditional Blocks

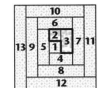
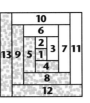

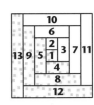

Make 9.
Pinks and creams
Heart

Make 5.
Aqua print
and golds
Bottom of gown

Make 5.
Golds and creams
Wing

Make 3.
Golds and aquas
Wing

Make 2.
Aqua print
and creams
Gown

Make 2.
Yellows
and creams
Wing

Make 1.
Aqua print
and pinks
Gown

Make 1.
Aqua print, golds
and yellows
Gown

Make 1.
Aqua print, aquas
and creams
Gown

Make 1.
Pinks, aqua print
and creams
Heart/Gown

Make 1.
Aqua print, golds
and creams
Gown/Wing

Courthouse Steps Blocks

Make 34
Aquas
Background

Make 30.
Aquas and creams
Scalloped
background

Make 21.
Creams
Background

Make 19.
Pinks
Heart

Make 12.
Aqua print
Gown

Make 9.
Golds and
yellows
Wing

Make 8.
Yellows and
golds
Wing

Make 1.
Golds
Wing

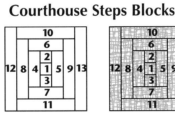

Color Key

| Creams | | Aquas | | Yellows | |
| Pinks | | Aqua print | | Golds | |

Materials: 44"- wide fabric

1⅞ yds. total assorted aquas for sky

1⅛ yds. total assorted creams for background

⅞ yd. aqua print for gown (different shade than sky aquas)

¾ yd. total assorted pinks for heart

⅝ yd. total assorted golds for wings, halo, hair, shoes, and inner bow

½ yd. total assorted yellows for wings and bow

½ yd. pink print for border

3 yds. for backing and binding

⅛ yd. skin-tone fabric for face, hands, and foot

Note: If you use lamé in your quilt, back it with interfacing.

Notions: dark brown, medium pink, and dark pink embroidery floss; fabric crayon or paint for angel's cheeks; 1 yd. gold cording for belt and hairbow (See photo.)

Directions

1. Color in the quilt plan and blocks with colored pencils to help eliminate mistakes.

2. Make a sample block to test the accuracy of your seam allowance. The block should measure 4" square (it will be 3½" square when sewn into the quilt).

3. Before making the blocks, be sure to reserve enough of the yellows and golds needed for the appliqué pieces.

4. Using either the speed-piecing method or templates, make blocks shown on page 79.

5. When all of the blocks are completed, sew the blocks together in horizontal rows. Then sew the rows together, making sure to match the seams between each block.

6. From the pink print, cut:
   2 strips, 2½" x 44", for border
   2 strips, 2½" x 58" (piece for length), for border
   Attach border strips to each side of the quilt and miter corners as shown on pages 84–85.

7. Using the templates (T-14 on the pullout patterns), complete the appliqué:
   face, halo, then hair to body
   hands to heart
   bow to heart
   foot, then shoe to bottom of gown

8. Complete the embroidery. See page 20 for embroidery stitches.
   fingers and nails—brown outline stitch
   eyes and nose—brown outline stitch
   upper lip—dark pink satin stitch
   lower lip—medium pink satin stitch with a line of brown outline stitch between the lips
   lines to indicate chest and arm—brown outline stitch
   lines in bow—brown outline stitch

9. Paint or color cheeks in soft pink.

10. Mark the top for quilting. Mark evenly spaced diagonal cross-hatch grid lines in heart and sky. Mark straight cross-hatch grid lines in cream background. Draw folds in the gown, and scallops in the wings and around the edges of the cream section.

11. Layer quilt top, batting, and backing. Pin or baste layers together. Quilt on all marked lines and around angel, bow, and heart.

12. When quilting is complete, trim batting and backing to match quilt top. Bind edges with 2½"-wide strips of fabric, using the double-fold method on pages 87–88.

13. Attach gold-cord belt and hairbow.

Note: The heart was designed with space for embroidering names and special dates, such as births, confirmations, or christenings.

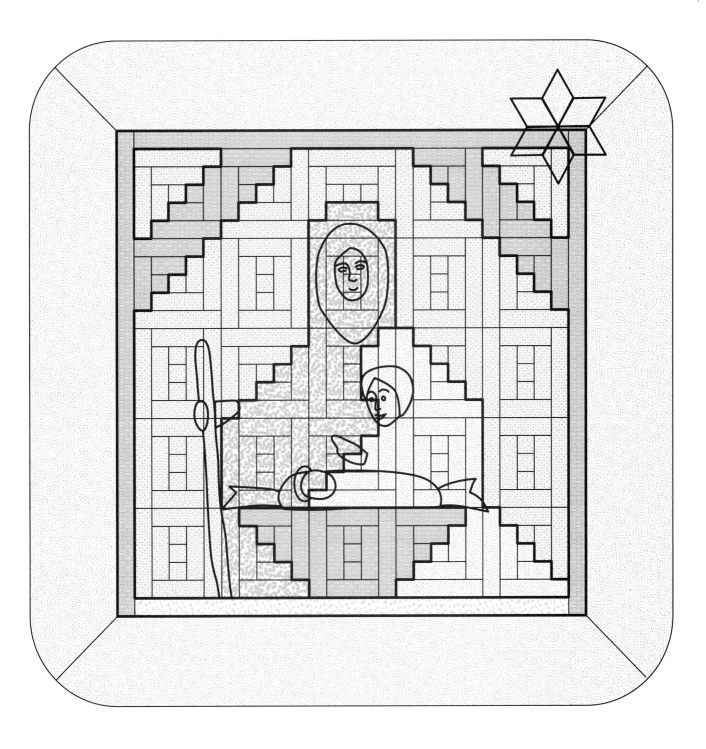

Photo: page 52 • Size: 19″ x 19″ • 25 Blocks • Block Size: 2¹/₂″ x 2¹/₂″

Traditional Blocks

Make 6.
Dk. blue
and brown
Stable

Make 2.
Lt. blue and
dk. blue
Mary/Sky

Make 1.
Lt. blue
and purple
Mary/Joseph

Make 1.
Dk. blue
and purple
Joseph/Sky

Make 1.
Purple and
brown
Joseph/Manger

Make 1.
Lt. blue and
brown
Mary/Manger

Courthouse Steps Blocks

Make 7.
Dk. blue
Sky

Make 2.
Purple
Joseph

Make 1.
Brown
Manger

Make 1.
Lt. blue
Mary

Make 1.
Purple and
lt. blue
Mary/Joseph

Make 1.
Purple and
dk. blue
Joseph/Sky

Color Key

Lt. blue ▢ Brown ▣ Gold ▢

Dk. blue ▢ Purple ▤

Materials: 44"- wide fabric

⅓ yd. light blue for Mary and border
¼ yd. dark blue for sky
¼ yd. brown for stable, manger, and hair
⅛ yd. purple for Joseph
1¼ yds. for backing and binding
Scraps of the following fabrics:
   Gold for hay and star
   Off-white for baby's blanket
   Skin-tone fabric for hands and faces
   Yellow for star

Notions: gold and brown embroidery floss; peach paint or fabric crayon for cheeks

Directions

1. Color in the quilt plan and blocks with colored pencils to help eliminate mistakes.
2. Make a sample block to test the accuracy of your seam allowance. The block should measure 3" square (it will be 2½" square when sewn into the quilt).
3. Using either the speed-piecing method or templates, make the blocks shown above.

4. When all the blocks are completed, sew the blocks together in vertical rows as shown in the quilt plan on page 81. Sew the rows together, making sure to match the seams between each block.

5. To complete the stable:
   a. Cut a 1" x 13" strip from gold; sew it to the bottom of the quilt.
   b. Cut a 1" x 13" strip from brown; sew it to the top of the quilt.
   c. Cut 2 strips, 1" x 14", from brown; sew one to each side of quilt.

6. From light blue, cut 4 strips, 3" x 20", for border. Attach border strips to each side of the quilt and miter corners as shown on pages 84–85.

7. Using the templates (T-15 on the pullout patterns), complete the appliqué:
   face, then hair and hand to Mary
   hay, then blanket, then baby to manger
   hand section A, then staff, then hand section B to Joseph
   beard, then face to Joseph

8. Piece star and appliqué to upper right hand corner of quilt top.

9. Complete the embroidery. See page 20 for embroidery stitches.
   all facial details—brown outline stitch (except pupils, which are brown satin stitch)
   Joseph's hand and nails—brown outline stitch
   baby Jesus's halo and blanket lines—gold outline stitch

10. Paint or color cheeks pink.

11. Mark the top for quilting as desired.

12. Layer quilt top, batting, and backing. Pin or baste layers together. Quilt on all marked lines and around all figures, manger, star, staff, and stable.

13. When quilting is complete, trim batting and backing to match quilt top. Round the 4 quilt corners, cutting through all 3 layers. Bind edges with 1½"-wide strip of continuous bias binding, overlapping ends. (See page 88.)

Finishing Techniques

❧ *Adding Borders*

Borders may be added one strip at a time, or strips for borders may be sewn together and then mitered.

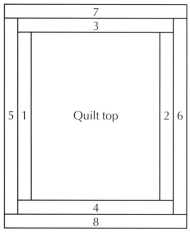

Add borders in numerical order.
It is like a giant Courthouse Steps Block.

Mitered Borders

1. Mark the center edges of the borders and design area by folding them in half and inserting a pin at the fold.
2. With right sides together, match borders to quilt top, following diagram. Pin in place at beginning and end of seam line. Be sure to match center pins.

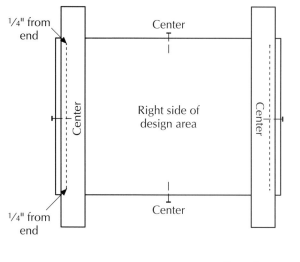

3. Stitch two borders in place on opposite sides, beginning and ending seams ¼" from ends.
4. Press seams toward the borders.
5. Repeat with remaining two borders. (Seams will begin and end at the ends of the two previously stitched border seams.) Anchor the seam points with a pin.
6. Working on one corner at a time, fold top border under to form a mitered corner.

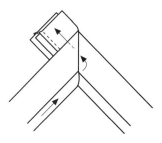

7. Align seam lines of border strips as indicated by arrows. Pin as shown. Press fold, remove pins, and press a firm crease at the fold.

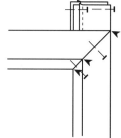

8. Leave pins in borders as shown.

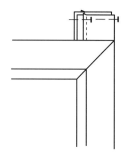

9. Fold borders with right sides together. Open seams and fold away from border. Insert pins through edges of border strips. Check underneath to see if pins are aligned with seams and adjust pins if necessary.

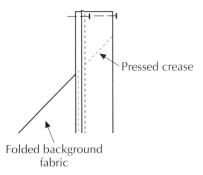

Pressed crease

Folded background fabric

10. Stitch on crease from design area to border edges. Trim excess ¼" away from seam.

Preparing to Quilt

1. Cut backing and batting several inches larger than quilt top. Spread the backing on a flat, clean surface, wrong side up; anchor it with pins or masking tape.

2. Position batting on top of backing. Place quilt top on top of batting. Baste all three layers together from the center to the outside corners and edges. Baste outer edges.

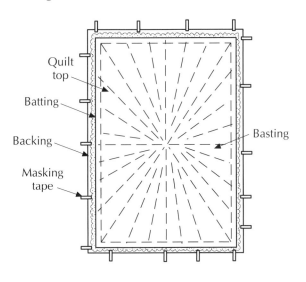

Quilt top

Batting

Backing

Masking tape

Basting

Quilting

Machine quilting works well on these Log Cabin quilts. There is much less marking to do than on other quilts because the blocks and pictures show you where to quilt. In "Humpty Dumpty" (page 28) for example, I simply quilted around each block, the egg, the castle, and the other shapes.

Because there are so many things to know about fine machine quilting, I recommend that you consult a book on the subject before attempting it. For best results when machine quilting, pin or tack layers together rather than basting. You may also need to use special thread, machine needles, machine feet, and flatter batting than usual.

After you pin-baste the quilt and make the necessary adjustments to your sewing machine, you are ready to begin. Quilt from the center and work out to the sides.

Some tips to help:

- The larger the quilt, the more difficult it is to handle in a sewing machine. Roll excess fabric inside the machine arm to make maneuvering easier.
- Remember to catch the bobbin thread and pull it up through the quilt top each time you begin to quilt in a new place. This prevents tangles on the quilt back.
- Check for correct tension on both the top and bottom of the quilt.
- Clear or light gray monofilament thread on the top eliminates the need to change thread colors.
- Use thread that matches the quilt back in the bobbin. Remove pins as you go if they are in your way.

Machine quilting takes practice, but it is well worth learning!

Suggestions for quilting designs are given with each pattern. I hand quilt most of my quilts, but these small Log Cabin blocks are difficult to hand quilt because of the many seams.

To quilt by hand, you will need:

quilting needles (I use the heavier, size 10 needles to get through the seams, and smaller needles in the border)

two thimbles (one for the middle finger of each hand), and two rubber fingers (to go inside thimbles and keep them from falling off)

quilting hoop (14"–18" diameter)

small scissors

quilting thread

Use a single thread no longer than 18". Make a small, single knot at one end of the thread. The quilting stitch is a small running stitch that goes through all three layers of the quilt. To begin, insert the needle in the top layer about ¾" from the point where you want to start stitching. Pull the needle out at the starting point and gently tug at the knot until it pops through the fabric and is buried in the batting. Make a backstitch through all three layers at the beginning of the quilting line. Proceed to quilt small, even stitches on the marked line until the thread is 5"–6" from the end. Then make a single knot close to the fabric. Make a backstitch to bury the knot in the batting. Run the thread off through the batting and out the quilt top and snip it off. Repeat until the quilting is completed.

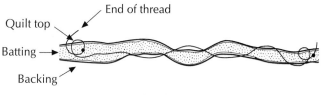

Hand quilting stitch

Important: Always begin quilting from the center of the quilt and work out. This will eliminate puckers. Make sure your backing is several inches larger than the quilt top to ensure there is enough fabric on the edges.

🦋 *Binding*

There are numerous ways to finish the edges of a quilt. For the patterns in this book, I have used self-made binding strips. Strips are sewn, one at a time, to sides, top, and bottom of the quilt through all three layers (quilt top, batting, and backing). This can be done by hand or by machine. Strips are then folded to the back and stitched in place by hand.

Regular Binding Method

1. Cut fabric strips the width stated in the individual projects. If strips are not long enough to fit the side of the quilt, piece the strips to the required length.
2. With right sides together, sew binding strips to the sides of the quilted project through all layers, using a ¼"-wide seam allowance.

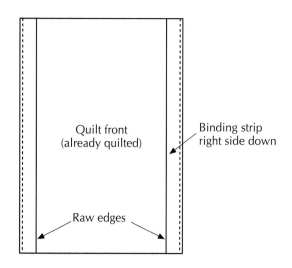

3. Open side bindings before sewing on top and bottom binding strips.

4. With right sides together, sew binding strips to top and bottom of quilt through all layers.

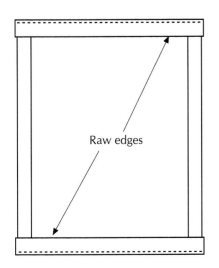

5. Bring the binding to the back of quilt. Fold raw edges under and blindstitch in place. Square corners or turn under corner for miter.

Fold raw edges under ¼".

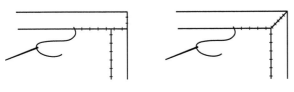

Square or miter corners.

Double-Fold Binding Method

This method requires twice the amount of fabric, because the binding is folded in half lengthwise before it is sewn to the quilt.

1. Cut fabric strips the width stated in the individual projects, piecing as necessary.
2. Fold the strip in half lengthwise, wrong sides together and press.

3. With right sides together, match raw edges of the binding and the quilt top. Sew binding to the sides of the quilt through all layers with a ¼"-wide seam.

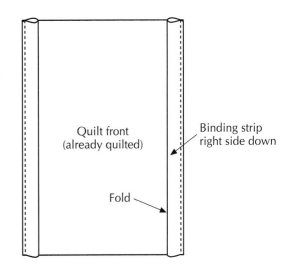

4. Open side bindings before sewing on top and bottom binding strips.
5. Sew binding to top and bottom of quilt.

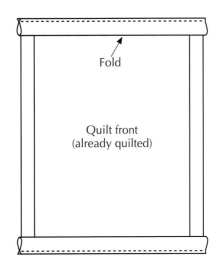

6. Bring the binding to the back and blindstitch in place. Square corners or turn under corner for miter.

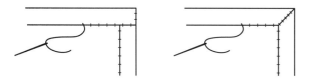

Square or miter corners.

Note: Sometimes a quilt binding is "continuous," as in the "Christmas Nativity" quilt on page 81. I made this binding from one continuous strip of fabric cut on the bias. (You can piece a continuous-binding strip to get the required length.) Trim the quilt corners to be softly rounded. Sew the bias strip all the way around the quilt until the ends overlap. Turn the raw edges to the quilt back, fold under $\frac{1}{4}$", and blindstitch in place.

About the Author

Christal Carter began quilting in 1979 and quickly discovered the design possibilities of the versatile Log Cabin block. She makes "picture quilts" and especially "Log Cabin picture quilts" her focus. She has designed many prizewinning quilts and has been the featured guest artist of five major quilt shows.

Christal self-publishes a line of quilt patterns and has written three books (published by That Patchwork Place). She is the owner of Majestic Seasons, a decorating firm that specializes in corporate theme parties.

Currently she is traveling internationally with her quilt collection, giving quilt lectures and workshops. Christal is a wife and the mother of two grown daughters. She makes her home in Southern California.